Final Witness

FINAL WITNESS

My Journey from the Holocaust to Ireland

Zoltan Zinn-Collis

with

Alicia McAuley

maverick house

First published in 2006 by

Maverick House Publishers, Main Street, Dunshaughlin, Co. Meath, Ireland.
Maverick House SE Asia, 440 Sukhumvit Road, Washington Square, Klongton,
Klongtoey, Bangkok 10110, Thailand.

info@maverickhouse.com
http://www.maverickhouse.com

ISBN: 1-905379-18-8
978-1-905379-18-7

5 4 3 2 1

The paper used in this book comes from wood pulp of managed forests. For every
tree felled at least one tree is planted, thereby renewing natural resources.

A CIP catalogue record for this book is available from the British
Library.

ZOLTAN'S JOURNEY

from Slovakia to Ireland
via Bergen-Belsen
concentration camp

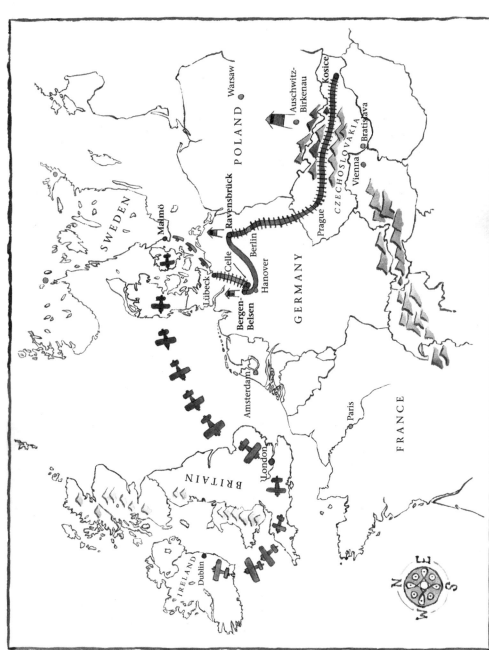

DEDICATION

———◆———

I HAVE IT ON GOOD AUTHORITY that it is customary, when one has written a book, to dedicate it to someone or something.

Just before I do that, I would like to thank my minder and spelling corrector in this endeavour. She has listened to me waffle, babble and answer questions she never even asked, at all times with a gentle smile and a rather bemused expression. We started off with one confused person; now we have two. But nonetheless, this is the beginning of a story, and between us we have managed to arrive at an end. Well done, Alicia. It could not have been easy.

I want to dedicate this work to my wife and daughters, for their support and help with it—even though they made it quite clear that they were glad to get me out from under their feet. 'Don't you have something to write?' has become the standard reply to any offer of household helpfulness since I began this book. There could not be many things worse than an old man in a precarious medical condition offering to help in things where he would be a definite hindrance, if not a direct danger to the health and safety of all concerned. So Siobhan, Caroline, Nichola, Emma and Joan, I forgive you for any slights or disparaging remarks against me, real or imagined.

This work is for the women in my life—my four daughters, and my wife, Joan, who gave them to me. In the five of you I have managed to create a new life, and latch on to some of that which circumstances forced me to miss out on for so many years. Of course, it has not all been walking hand in hand down the golden way, smelling the flowers as we passed by. For heaven's sake, we are a family. We have had our rows. I have demanded to know where you were going and with whom, when you were coming back, and how. I have embarrassed you, as a daddy does. I have been such a mean daddy, hated, never to be spoken to again.

And looking back, it has been wonderful.

Now four males have come into this, my family. Two grandsons and one granddaughter have also appeared, and have made it more wonderful still.

Yeats, Beckett, Joyce and the rest of you, you are safe in your positions. You will not be eclipsed by my few lines. But to me they matter. They have issued from my heart to the ones I love, and I hope they will tell my family some of the things I find hard to say face to face. When you girls bring me or my ashes up to Bo, I want you to remember what is contained in these pages, because it is for you. As the world goes around, so do human lives and the families that make them. And as my little life goes around, remember that you lot, you are what made me.

Zoltan Zinn-Collis
April 2006

FOREWORD

———————

'YOU'RE TWO MINUTES LATE,' ZOLTAN DECLARED, tapping his watch and peering at me sceptically. I was surprised—it was our first meeting after all—but I would soon learn to take his reproaches less seriously. A mordant pronouncement, I would discover, is his usual way of meeting strangers. This was simply par for the course.

On that occasion he was wearing a tasteful yet striking Winnie the Pooh tie. I remarked upon it, and he lifted his trouser leg to reveal a matching sock. 'My knickers,' he informed me with a characteristic grin, 'are my own business.'

For Zoltan, such excursions into childhood are common, and childhood is a recurring theme with him. He claims a real affinity with young people: when I met him he had just been to speak in a secondary school—something he has done regularly since, 50 years after his liberation, he began to speak about his experiences in the Bergen-Belsen concentration camp. He makes no bones about the fact that he relishes the opportunity to reclaim, albeit vicariously, some of the childhood experience that was so banefully wrenched from under his own feet. Hence the tie, socks and—legend has it—the knickers.

But this relish in childhood is not an escape or a denial. Attached to the Winnie the Pooh tie he wears an anti-racism pin—a more subtle but equally powerful sign, which tells us that when Zoltan flirts with childhood he does not forget his adult concerns. He wears his Holocaust experience as a badge, and if it has caused him to find solace in other childhoods, it has also left him with a very adult sense of responsibility. In private he is a family man, and has deliberately protected his wife and children from his own emotional baggage; but in public Zoltan is a Holocaust survivor—a relentless ambassador for the forces that have kept him alive through one of the darkest hours of history. He is a man on a mission, determined to testify to what he has witnessed.

The distortion of his spine by the tuberculosis he contracted in Belsen has left him exceptionally short, and he is likely to become more so in the coming years. He now walks haltingly and with great effort and must keep to a strict and limited diet because of his diabetes. There is a good chance, too, that he will end his days totally paralysed from the waist down. (Typically, Zoltan will brook no expression of pity and greets any attempt at such with a conversation-stopping, 'Shit happens.')

But the psychological scars of his experience are scarcely less evident than the physical. He is so wary of human contact that he is never first to offer his hand for the shaking; he abhors busy pubs and restaurants; he carefully avoids letting himself be caught in a crowd. And more strikingly, he cultivates a distinctive brusqueness of manner. Zoltan has no time for the conventions of self-conscious politeness and will say what is on his mind no matter who is listening. This, to say the least, can be off-putting, but it allows Zoltan to maintain around himself an emotional exclusion zone. If you cannot come close enough, physically and emotionally, you cannot hurt him.

But there is more to Zoltan's curt demeanour. As well as maintaining his own defences in social situations it allows him to penetrate those of other people, the inevitable protective husks of small talk and pretension. Despite his detachment, his humour is as incisive as a scalpel and can cut, without ceremony, to the bone. The persona he presents means that he can advance towards and retreat from human contact at will—and that is crucial, since, essentially, the function of this persona is not protection, but control. Zoltan has been crushed among the dead and the dying in fetid cattle trucks and concentration camps, and thereby robbed brutally of any control of physical and mental contact with other people. He has had his space invaded in the most horrific fashion, with the effect that it is now of paramount importance for him to be in complete control of his own body and the space around it—at all times, and at much cost.

Zoltan is fully aware of his adult mistrust of human

contact, and of the fact that his childhood experience in the cattle trucks and in Belsen is at its core. He can talk about this and the many comparable phenomena in his adult life with acceptance and apparent detachment. This is a measure, if one were needed, not only of his astuteness but also of his magnanimity. He is willing to separate himself and his experience, to look at both as objectively as possible and to ask, 'What are these effects, these defences? What am I, and how much of what I am was made by Adolf Hitler? To what extent am I involved in this thing called history? And, perhaps most importantly, what is my responsibility to it?'

The answers to these questions are not easily found, because the effects of the Holocaust on any one of its living victims are immeasurably deep and intricate. Self-analysis, especially when it must break down a lifetime's worth of psychological fortifications, is a difficult business. As Zoltan points out, he does not deserve to be lauded for surviving the Holocaust. What enabled him to do so was not his own merit or ability, but good luck and the goodwill of others. But in giving his difficult testimony he has been honest, and for that he deserves immense credit.

Zoltan is a man of contradictions. He is at once a skilful manipulator of human relationships and an aloof loner; he uses humour both to protect his own psyche and to penetrate it. He is at the same time the arch egotist and the good Samaritan. The fact that he calls himself the Slovak Irish Paddy illustrates the paradox. Zoltan is one concerned with getting on with the business of being an Irishman, but at the same time consumed with the knowledge that the Holocaust is something we must never forget. He has written his account for the sake of his mother, father, brother, sister and the millions of others whom the Nazis murdered. But he has also written it because laying down what the Holocaust has done to him may help to purge the memory and bring him some relief from the effects of his experience. Let us hope that this will be the case.

Alicia McAuley
April 2006

PROLOGUE

———✦———

I HAVE BEEN ASKED ON NUMEROUS occasions, by numerous people, when and if I am going to write my autobiography. 'Why?' I have always thought. Is it that they fear my early demise? Do they want to know what I think of them? I would have thought that to be worthy of such a work it would be necessary to be in some way special—to have achieved something of note in my time. I have not climbed any mountains, crossed any deserts, painted any great pictures or composed any breathtaking music. I have not built an orphanage in the Balkans or helped resolve any of the numerous conflicts on this troubled planet of ours. I am not a particularly good man; I am not even a particularly bad man.

To put down on paper your life's paltry struggles, joys and sorrows for others to dissect, pore over, interpret, analyse and parse—and then rubbish—seems to me to be the height of conceit.

And yet. Although I am not an extraordinary man, I have had an extraordinary experience—and I do feel that I must articulate it. With the greatest of ill luck, I was taken to places of great suffering, and things were done to me that should never have been done to anyone. I was robbed of my childhood, and almost destroyed by the utmost evil. And with the greatest of good fortune, I was picked up when I fell down, and put together again when I was broken. I made a fool of medical science and evaded death several times. I found new loves and even regained a childhood through my own children.

I am one of the millions who went through the Nazi concentration camps, but I differ from most of them in that I managed to come out alive, and more or less intact.

So perhaps with whatever humility I can find in me, for I am not as humble as I should be, I ought to put my 'yet' down on paper. Perhaps I ought to tell all that happened to me, and try to give an insight into what it is to be a displaced person, a refugee, a survivor of what was called the Final Solution.

By doing so I may be able to make the people who were not there to see it aware of what we, as people, are capable of doing to each other in the name of who knows what—for the same thing is happening today. The numbers nowadays are not so vast, and systems are not so organised, but for those who happen to go to worship on the wrong day of the week, have the wrong shaped eyes or the wrong coloured skin, the outcome is the same. Perhaps in some way I may be able to speak for the millions who did not survive and have no one else to speak for them. Already, there goes my humility. But who has more right to speak for these dead than one who bore witness to their destruction?

I am proud. Proud that I have survived against the odds—not because of anything I did myself, but by the grace of that multi-named being some of us call God, and by the goodwill of a series of extraordinary people. In telling my story, I hope that I will be able to thank them, and to put back some of what has been given to me.

And then I will have achieved something—something that may, in the end, be just as valuable as climbing a mountain or crossing a desert. I hope that it will make us aware of ourselves and of our place in things, and that it will help us to realise that no matter what the colour of our eyes or the shape of our nose, we are no different from anybody else. Like everybody else, we have to eat and sleep and break wind, we have to have and to give love. And you never know—I may also be able to put some of my own ghosts to rest.

Some memories may have gone for good; some details I must draw from the written accounts of my new father, comprised of facts he gathered from me when I was still a child. But everything told here is true. There will be evil and brutality, butchery and barbarity in my story, for that was the nature of the Holocaust. That is what I witnessed. Yet this must not be a tale of woe and sorrow. After all that was inflicted by one group of people came another group of people—who gave and showed the very opposite side of human nature: its compassion, its comfort and its capacity to love. They had the courage to say, 'Stop,' to stand up against evil and to redress the balance in my life. In the end, the hero arrived, got the girl, and rode into the sun on his white horse. Happiness reigned.

So I will sit down at my computer and begin to bash out the story of my life—or, perhaps, of my nine lives, since I seem to be as good at escaping death as a cat. Cats and I, in fact, have a lot in common, and they will slink into this story quite a lot. Some time ago, my youngest daughter came home from school with a thing in a plastic bag, which turned out to be a kitten—eyes just open, not yet able to drink. He was presented to me with a 'do something' look. I fed him baby food with a medical syringe and named him Gizmo. He now thinks I am his mother and, despite my asthma, claims rights to my bed. But I love him and he loves me. My wife is not too keen on him, but I think the feeling is mutual, so I suppose that is all right. We have become inseparable, which has been his choice, not mine. It must have been great baby food. At the moment we are sharing the chair I am sitting on. He has the bigger half.

I know from the distant past in school that a story should have a beginning, a middle and an end—for preference, in that order—so I will begin at the beginning. With a bit of luck I will manage to get to a middle and then to an end—and I hope that neither you nor I will get too confused along the way.

PART ONE

———————

THE BEGINNING

the flesh? it was melted away,
the heart burnt out, dead ember,
tendons, muscles shattered, outer husk dismembered,

yet the frame held:
we passed the flame: we wonder
what saved us? what for?

—H.D., 'The Walls Do Not Fall'

MY STORY BEGINS AMONG THE FOOTHILLS of the High Tatra, in what is now called Slovakia, and was then the eastern part of Czechoslovakia. I was born in August 1940. I do not know the exact date, but I have settled on the first, which is, after all, as good as any other.

I know very little indeed about my family. At the end of the Second World War, the man who became my new father gathered what information he could from the two miserable orphans he had found in a concentration camp and brought with him back to Ireland, and did his best to record it. He also went to Slovakia and found our grandmother, who told him the rest. Most of the memories we gave him have long since become muddled and uncertain in my mind. What I can tell you of my family's life among the snowy hills of Slovakia is partly second-hand, but none the less true.

My father was a Slovak Jew of no great means. He was a sometime painter and decorator, although I have a feeling that the sometimes were none too frequent. I think I can say he was tall, but then everybody is tall to a four-year-old, so that probably does not mean a great deal. I am certain, though, that he had dark hair which was going a little salt-and-pepper, and a salt-and-pepper moustache.

My mother was of Hungarian origin, from a cultured Protestant background and genteel poverty. She had black hair, which she wore in a bob. About her appearance, strangely, I have no clearer idea than that, even though she was with us right up until we were liberated from Nazi hands.

Neither family, apparently, had been very keen on their marriage. My father's family saw in his intended bride a cultured young woman, but a Gentile; my mother's family saw a handsome young man, but a poor one. A Jew, too. Even in this remote place there was an inkling that the Jews were about to get it in the neck, yet again. But my mother and father were both stubborn, or foolish, or very much in love, and they married anyway. I like to think it was love alone—and since there's no one left to stop me, I will.

They had four children—my sister Edit, my brother Aladar, myself and a baby girl, whose name I do not know. Edit was two and a half years older than me, and Aladar was older than me by about a year. We lived in the cottage of my mother's mother, in a rural hamlet not unlike any you might find in Ireland, where I ended up. Everybody knew their neighbours' business, right down to what they had for dinner—and had no qualms about talking about it. It was a small community like any other. There was the usual geniality and warmth, the usual friendships and family attachments, but there were also the usual rivalries, resentments and trivial disputes. As it happened, when the opportunity came for us to be betrayed to the Nazis, petty differences like these would be our undoing.

We had an Alsatian by the name of Rolf—a great big slob of a dog, whom I loved. Rolf and Aladar and I would be three puppies together, in a heap, all over the place. There was a cat, too—a tom, I think—who was great friends with my elder sister. They used to be able to sense each other's presence. If you saw one, the other usually wasn't far behind. I think the cat was called Marus. Marus was the first of the many cats in my tale.

That was my family: Granny, Father, Mother, Edit, Aladar, me, my baby sister, Rolf and the cat. Eight, and now there are only two of us.

I cannot really tell what our day-to-day life was like. I have the facts, but the experience I have forgotten. However, there are a few disparate moments of memory that for one reason or another remain clear as day in my mind. As my life was turned upside down and all sorts of horrible things began to happen to me, my childish mind packed these episodes in ice and carried them across Europe—as a reminder of the past, perhaps, from a time when things were good. As it turned out, these memories were a keepsake I would treasure throughout my life.

I can remember, for example, sitting around a big kitchen table one evening. I was at one end, my black-haired mother was at the other and Edit was on my left, seeming very small in a big wooden chair. My father and Aladar were painting a picture of a window on a wall. It was magnolia. Even there and at that time, magnolia. Someone was calling them to the table. It was my mother, who was handing out thick slices of bread and dripping, with sugar dusted on top. My father took one and sprinkled it not with sugar, but with salt and pepper from the small wooden bowls on the table, because he was a grown-up. I watched Mother as she cut a smaller slice for my youngest sister, smoothly sliding the blade of the knife through the tines of the fork. She saw that I was watching, and smiled at me gently.

I can also remember my birthday, my fourth. I had been given a toy trumpet. It was red, blue and gold, and for me a thing of great beauty and wonder. I was playing with it in the back garden of our house. I had never seen a trumpet before, and worked out, with some effort, that if you blew into one end a sound came out the other—albeit not a very musical sound. Looking around me, I spied the tap attached to the brick wall at the back of the garden. I was an inquisitive boy even then, and I wondered what would happen if I put water into the blowing end. Perhaps a different kind of noise would come out. I gave it a try.

Nothing came out—except a sad wet trickle, and I went running to Mother in dismay. Instead of sympathy, though, I got a clip around the ear for breaking my new trumpet. Looking back at that incident, I think that a pat on the back might have been more in order. I must have made quite a racket with that thing, and now, because of my experiment, it was quite silent. Grown-ups can be quite ungrateful at times.

There was a little boy about the same age as myself who lived in the house on the other side of the brick wall. Like me, he was frequently to be found playing in the garden. One morning, for no reason I can recall, he lobbed a brick over the wall. I didn't notice it until it was much too late to get out of the way, and it landed with a dull crunch on my foot. The surprise of this, never mind the pain, sent me howling in to Mother once again. This time I did get some sympathy but, being a proud Hungarian, she told me to go straight out and throw it back. With a fierce cry I hurled the brick as high as I could, with as much force as my little arms could manage. But I was very small, the wall was very tall, and the brick was very heavy. It clipped the edge of the wall, went into a high backward spin and landed, crunch, on my other foot. I howled. I have been told I was very good at howling, though now I just moan like a grumpy old man. I have the walking stick; I just need to get the flat cap.

Beside the brick wall there was a wooden outhouse and an outdoor toilet. It was the only toilet we had, although I am pretty sure that to have any sort of proper toilet in those days was the exception rather than the rule. I remember that in the outhouse there was a gun belonging to one of my uncles, which mesmerised and frightened me in equal measure. One day my uncle took it and shot a hole right through the thick wooden door of the toilet. I was stunned—what a powerful instrument it must be that could do such a thing. I stayed away from it after that, although before long I would be forced to learn a lot more about guns and their power.

I was too young to go to school at that time, but for some reason Edit took me with her one day. I can remember coming home full of excitement and plonking myself down in a chair. 'Look what I learned to do!' I shouted. Awkwardly, but ostentatiously, I folded my arms. This was not met with the raucous applause I expected, but rather with complete indifference from everyone in the room. The grown-ups, evidently, were talking about grown-up things. I cannot remember what happened next—but no doubt, I howled.

Another time, we three older children had just been to see *Snow White* in the nearest town. It was the first film I had ever seen. I was still frightened, because the witch had been very evil. But the journey home was by train. I had never been on a train before, and was thrilled—so much so that I soon completely forgot about witches who talked to their mirrors and destroyed innocent girls with poison. We had a carriage all to ourselves. I can remember watching the countryside go by in a bright blur and thinking about how fast we must be going. The door of the noisy carriage had a window, and you could raise and lower it with a leather strap. This fascinated me, and I inspected it with wonder all the way home.

When we came bounding along the road that led to my family's house that day, we found that on both sides of the road had appeared large grey monsters with pointed snouts—artillery pieces.

And that is all. These memories play, and the screen goes dark in my mind as if a film reel had just run out. I have some impressions of feeling, some dull ideas of shapes and smells, but nothing else from this time that I can really call memory.

I have said that I would not let all this be wailing and weeping, feeling sorry for myself. I won't—because I do not feel sorry for myself. How can I? I am alive when millions just like me are not. Yet I think I must try to explain, if I can, what it is like to know that you had a family, and that now you don't. I do not know them, and yet they knew me. I cannot say with honesty that it is a feeling of loss. What I have lost I did not really know. Nor is it grief exactly. And yet, I have this feeling of having missed out on something. I have a new home, a new family, a new country and a new life. I am alive, and I am happy. So what is missing?

Wouldn't I be the clever one if I knew the answer to that? Possibly what I think I am talking about is a feeling of no past. I wasn't born; I came from under a gooseberry bush. I cannot remember my uncles, my cousins, my birthdays, my special treats and little punishments—I have almost nothing of where I come from—of my heritage, although I hate that word. The history of my Slovak childhood as I know it is the information our new father gathered from my sister and me, but which I, for the most part, have long since forgotten. The Nazis not only robbed me of my family, but also of my past. I am *The Man with No Name*.

In general, I do not dwell on this. I do not indulge these thoughts. But if I am feeling a bit low for whatever reason, and feel the need to suck worms, this 'alone' comes over me. The people who adopted me are my family. I am grateful to them beyond measure, because it is thanks to them that I am still here. But when they took me in they made me into someone new—someone who feels, and perhaps is, different. If that is a good way to feel and be, I have no idea. Let someone else decide that. But it certainly feels odd at times.

When I was five years old and I told my new father about the short life I had lived until then, I was in some way shedding it, divesting myself of my old existence as if it was a suit of worn-out clothes. This was necessary, I think. And I think it was good. I had a new life and had to get on with being Irish. But it meant that I had to cast off my own nationality and origin, and for that I feel some regret.

Perhaps as a consequence, it is difficult, at times even painful, to recall and put down the few memories I can still claim as my own—because they, too, might eventually slip out of my grasp. I know that these things happened to me. I was there, and this is my home and my family I am speaking about. With an effort of memory, I can see Aladar and my father painting the wall. Yet this is what was taken away from me, and I can never reclaim it.

All the same, I can take comfort in the idea that at that time I was oblivious to the awful things that were about to befall me and my family. I was happy. Why shouldn't I have been? I was a four-year-old boy. I ran around, got into trouble, got picked up, kissed better and then ran around some more. I had a warm bed to go to, food to eat, somebody to tell me what to do and when to do it. Family, comfort, routine, and love—when you have all these things, then what are the events that will make history?

The answer to that question would soon visit me most violently. By now Hitler's armies had swept across central Europe. The ordinary people of the countries they conquered were falling victim in their millions to Nazi strategy. Hitler's plan to bring about the supremacy of the Aryan race by eliminating anyone who was different was silently but surely being carried out. And my family was under its threat.

Slovakia had even since before my birth been under Nazi occupation; I had been born into the war.[1] But by the time the artillery pieces appeared along the road the adults were more and more often grave and subdued. I have an impression that they talked in hushed urgent tones, and had little time for small boys. I think my sister, too, was quieter, seeming to understand their mood, if not the reasons for it.

As the winter went on, I heard words like 'Jews,' 'Aryan' and 'Gestapo' spoken more and more often. I did not know what they meant, but the adults always whispered them—and in Hungarian, the language we used when things were serious. It seemed, because of the reverential, almost awed way they said them that these words had some secret power. I soon became afraid of them.

What I did not understand was that their fear was growing every day. My father was a Jew—and as far as the Nazis were concerned, so were his children. Jews were being rounded up and taken away; dark rumours abounded in our country about where they went and what was being done with them there. The time came when the adults of my family decided that something had to be done.

One morning, I found my mother busy packing clothes and dry food into a beaten old rucksack. 'Are we going away?' I asked her. She did not look up, but went on folding with the same slow, deliberate movements—scarcely seeming to notice her small and demanding son in the doorway, and certainly not paying me the attention I was looking for.

Later that day, my father arrived into the good room, where the family was gathered. We all ate a meal together during which scarcely a word was spoken. Nobody was talking or even looking at each other, and my sister frowned at me when I began to chuckle and wanted to play as usual. I knew they were sad, but I didn't know what it was about, and anyway, it didn't have anything to do with me.

After the meal, my father picked up the beaten rucksack, kissed each of us once, and left through the back door of the house. That was the last we would see of him for months. As he walked away, my mother looked out the small window in the door towards the foothills of the Tatra mountains. The trees at the edge of the steep, sloping woods were beginning to shed their foliage, and the brown leaves already covered the ground. My father steadily marched out through them. Crunch, crunch, crunch.

———•———

When my father decided to go into the woods to hide, it was for the best of reasons. I think it was at Uncle Peter's suggestion. Being well educated, he probably had a clearer idea of the danger we all faced than the rest of my family did. In fact, some of the family did not think a lot of my father for leaving us and going into hiding. It was well known that deportations of large numbers of people to the west were going on, as they had been since the early years of the war, but the concentration camps and gas chambers were still rumours, and vague ones at that. To leave one's family on the strength of such things was cowardice, it was said. Anyway, the Russians were every day moving westward, and would surely arrive before long.

The Russians were indeed advancing, and by the winter of 1944 the Reich was falling to pieces; its final defeat was only a matter of time. But despite, or perhaps because of this, the Nazis in Slovakia were determined to see through their last purge of the Slovak Jews—and Adolf Zinn, my father, was being hunted.

One day, several men with rifles appeared at our door. I think it was someone's birthday, because we had been eating a huge pink cake. It was not my birthday, but I had managed to get the biggest piece as usual. On the rare occasions when I did not get my way I spoke not the Slovak tongue of my father, nor the German of my uncle, but the funny Hungarian language of my grandmother. That made her love me even more and I could usually wriggle my way into her good books.

Being a bold little boy, the men didn't frighten me at all, but my sister Edit seemed to find something terrifying about them, especially the man with the round face who seemed to be in charge. They went into every room in the house— emptying drawers, peering into cupboards, rifling through bookshelves and piles of newspapers, ignoring the children and pets scampering around their feet. Finally, not having found whatever they had been looking for, they gathered around the kitchen table.

They began to speak to my mother gently in German. I didn't understand all of what they said, but the name Adolf Zinn was mentioned over and over. And there were those words again. Despite his calmness the man in charge spat slightly when he uttered them: 'Jew', 'purity', 'race', 'the Führer'. My mother had been gracious and smiling, even as they searched the house, but now her face became rigid, her expression defiant, her head held high. I noticed other words occurring again and again: 'Hungarian', 'mistake', 'annulled'.

The man in charge, I later discovered, was a German, a commandant of the local guardists, and had come all the way out to this backwater of the country to try to talk some sense into my mother. He knew she had married young, perhaps too young to know any better, and could see by the way she lived that she was obviously a hard-working woman—a good woman, from good Hungarian stock. Surely now that the abominable nature of the Jews had been revealed she felt differently about her marriage? Surely now that the world knew about the terrible and insidious danger they posed she had realised it had been a mistake? They would ruin the racial purity of good Aryan people, he told her. A woman like her shouldn't have thrown herself away on one of these vile, base Jews. Surely she realised that?

But it was not too late, he told her. No, by no means. The Reich was always ready to accept apologies. All she had to do was to come to the town hall and sign a piece of paper. Her marriage would be annulled and there would be no consequences for herself. The children, strictly speaking, were Jews too by the Reich's official definition, but even they would be let off the hook if she performed this simple task.

My mother showed no sign of changing her attitude. She stared at the man without flinching. 'No,' was all she said.

Seeing that he was not yet getting through to this stubborn

woman, the commandant changed his tone. Did she realise the consequences of her refusal to see sense? The fugitive was bound to be discovered eventually, and she knew what would happen then. He was a Jew after all—only a Jew—and self-evidently did not merit this kind of loyalty. Would she reconsider, for God's sake?

'No,' my mother said again.

The commandant was baffled. He began to think that perhaps this woman did not have the intelligence he had given her credit for. By now he sounded exasperated.

'But why on earth not?' he asked her.

She replied in a quiet but firm voice: 'Because I love him.'

The commandant was silent for a moment. He recognised in her the backbone of the Hungarian people, and realised that she was not to be persuaded. It was no use in pressing the matter further; anyway, he had other work to do. It was a pity, he must have thought, but fraternising with Jews will have its consequences.

The commandant's demeanour at once became cold and stiff. He stood up from the table, no longer a supplicant but an officer of the Reich, and looking my mother in the eye, he laid it on the line.

'When your husband is captured,' he said, 'you and your four children will be taken as Jews and deported.'

With that he marched out of our house, leaving my mother alone. I could see that she was trembling. She sat down slowly, and buried her face in her hands.

For months my father lived in the freezing forests; waiting, listening and knowing that sooner or later they were going to find him. He was a decorator after all, and didn't have the skills to live off the land. He became hungry, wet and bitterly cold. And worst of all, he became bitterly, bitterly lonely. As each day passed, he began to miss the company of other people, and his wife and children in particular. And that was what got to him. Eventually, unable to stand the isolation any longer, he left his camp and wandered into the town.

He came to an inn, in which some local men were discussing the situation. The arrival of the Russians, they were saying, was so close now that everybody was thinking of ways to show their gratitude.

'Stefan's wife is embroidering a hammer and sickle on her red petticoat!' one of them remarked.

My father had intended just to watch, but he couldn't help joining in with their laughter. Noticing for the first time his hunched form in a shadowy corner of the inn, the men became suspicious. Who was this stranger? Had anyone seen him before? He might be an informer. He must be—why else was he behaving so furtively? He would turn them in to the Gestapo—if they didn't stop him.

They confronted him. My father tried to escape, and tried to avoid their questions. But he was not a natural liar, and could not think of a believable explanation for who he was and what he was doing here. The men would not accept the vague and evasive excuses he offered. If he was not an informer, why would he not tell them who he was? They held him and drew him into a fight. The scuffle turned into a brawl, and moved out onto the street. People began to stop and watch. Someone called the local guardists, and they soon appeared.

It seems that then, one of the onlookers saw their chance. He recognised my father as a Jew on the run. Perhaps he believed the crude Nazi propaganda; perhaps, not realising the consequences, he wanted to settle an old score. Whatever the reason, he told the guardists my father's name, and my father was arrested and taken away.

Several days afterwards, we saw our father again. The Slovak guardists had handed him in to their superiors and he had been taken to the local Nazi headquarters. There he had been cast into a pitch-black, freezing-cold cell and left for hours. They had questioned him, relentlessly. They had tied him up. They had struck him and struck him again. They had pummelled his right foot with their heels until the bones had shattered. They had threatened to do still more horrific and vicious things to him, things so wildly cruel that even to hear them spoken made him cry out. And worse, they had threatened to do the same things to us, his family.

Finally, my father had given in. Yes, he was Adolf Zinn. Yes, he was a fugitive Jew. Yes, he was the husband of the Hungarian woman they had visited, and the father of her four young children.

When they brought him back to us we were all in the good room again—Mother, a coven of aunts, Uncle Peter, and Granny, of course. It was the same German commandant who had visited us before, and he was with one other guardist. My father was beaten and bloodied, limping painfully. When they dragged him in everyone gasped, and some of the aunts began to weep. Even though I was only four, I could see that there was deep pain in his eyes, which must have been both physical and mental.

The commandant no longer made any pretence at civility towards my mother. He became a beast, swearing and shouting at her and striking my father again. Whether or not this was for show, in front of the audience of his colleague and the assembled family, I do not know, but at that time it really did not matter to us. Aladar and I started to howl, and Edit tried desperately to hide behind Granny's skirts.

Coldly, they told my mother what was happening. They had come to take us away. They ordered my mother to pack one bag for us all, which would be all we were allowed to bring.

She did so and was back down in a few minutes. There were some very quick goodbyes. Then, my father made an effort to take charge. He tried to straighten his back, pick up the bag and lead his wife and frightened, shivering children out the door after the commandant. He was head of the family after all and, realising that he could not change what was to happen, he wanted to stand and be counted. I am proud of that memory. There were some good things that happened, even in this jumble of horrors.

However, with the beating he had received, he was not strong enough to carry the case. It fell to the ground and remained there—and as it fell, he winced with pain and shame. It is of little matter, though, that my father failed to lead us out of our house. The important thing to me is that he had mettle enough to make the attempt.

Mother was holding on to the baby and trying to get the rest of us moving as well, the bag still on the floor of the hallway. Eventually, to the disgust of the commandant, the young Slovak guardist picked it up sheepishly and carried it. But, evidently fearing that he would be seen by his superior to be sympathetic to this Jew and his mule of a wife, he prodded my father in the back, not as gently as he might have.

The aunts were in a very agitated state by this time and a few words of protest issued from one or two of them—but not too loudly. Granny, I know, just sat there and watched, her clear eyes wide and her body motionless. It could be that she had a good idea of what was to come and, while it pained her, she knew that it was something she could not defer or prevent. A granny, while saying nothing, can be very wise.

That was the last I saw of her, and of the rest of my extended family, and I know nothing more about them. I wonder what became of my brave granny and my cultured uncle Peter.

And the aunts. Where did they come from, and where did they go? Were they older or younger than my mother and father? Did they have husbands and children, lives of their own? I think they came from my mother's side, and I know there were a lot of them. I can remember their legs—some fat, some thin, under their skirts—some short, some long. When you are four and a half you don't see much over knee height. As we were led away they all clucked like hens when the fox is on the rampage. Thinking back on it now, that is rather what it was—except that the fox had two legs and wore a Nazi uniform.

I wonder if my mother knew what she was letting us all in for when she stood up so proudly against the guardist commandant. Did she realise that, in declaring her love for my father, she was putting that value ahead of life itself? In refusing to sign that piece of paper, she condemned herself, her husband and two of her children to death, and the other two to mortal danger and devastating loss.

I wish I could say that I was sure my mother didn't know what she was doing. If she was unaware of the consequences of refusing to sign that document, then her unflinching, noble loyalty does credit to her memory; and that way, it would be easy to forgive her. If she did know, on the other hand, then she valued love above our very lives—but that, perhaps, is nobler still. Either way, what is done is done, and the choice she made is not to be reversed. I could say that I forgive you, Mother, but there is no need. I never blamed you.

———•———

We were taken to the main hall of what must have been the nearest town of any size. It was now December 1944, the purge was well under way, and that town was being used as an assembly point for the deportees of the surrounding countryside. There were already a few families in the hall when we arrived. They all waited, in palpable dread, for the next bit of the journey to begin. The hall was long, bare and very cold, and had rows of hard trestle beds. By no means was it crowded, but one of the guards motioned that we were to settle ourselves in a bunk of two beds—all six of us.

That night, even now, seemed to have been a very long one. I remember that all of us children had a good go at howling. The babies were crying, and the mothers were trying to hold the whole thing together. As for the men, I am sure in my mind that they looked serious, exchanged views, opinions and ideas, probably used long words, and left the minding of the children to the women. I could say as usual, so I will. As usual.

Our mother was doing her best to pretend that everything was usual, that there was nothing to fear. It seemed to us like a trip to the doctor or to the home of a distant relative. We could sense the nervousness of the adults but, like all children, preferred to trust our mother's protection. She did her best to make us comfortable in the bunks and we slept fitfully.

Early in the morning, or perhaps later in the night—I don't know, because it was dark—we were called. We were given some breakfast, which I think consisted of ersatz coffee and bitter black bread, and herded outside. It was extremely cold.

They had told us to stay in an orderly group, but we children, having got out after quite some time cooped up, were running around, making noise and playing games, as children always will. This made our mothers deeply anxious, for despite the confusion that beleaguered us all, they must have had a good idea what would happen if we became too much of a nuisance. They hissed at us fretfully, trying ever more desperately to exert some control. The men moved a little bit away, and I suppose looked for even longer words and better arguments to trump each other with. This, of course, is understandable. Faced with the unknown, we all have a tendency to try to make sense of it, no matter how vain the attempt must be.

The walk from the town hall was weird. All the doors of the houses were shut. There was no one on the street, and no one looking out. I suppose that by this time, the people had seen the same thing happen so many times, it had lost its novelty.

I also have an idea, though, that there was probably a good deal of guilt involved. It is well recorded that a lot of old scores were settled by anonymous calls to the Gestapo. It may just have been that someone wanted a bit of land, a house, or perhaps a shop—and in that case it was easy to say the owner was a Jew, a suspected homosexual, or perhaps of gypsy extraction. It was not only racial hatred for which people were betrayed. Envy, greed, a desire for revenge—all the vices that normally make people bad neighbours—now made them executioners. Who knows why the person who recognised my father betrayed him to the Gestapo? Perhaps my father had done him some petty wrong; perhaps he simply owned more cattle.

At any rate, there was an eerie hush over the town that morning. We marched on until we reached what must have been the town square, where we were shoved and bundled into loose rows. We waited and waited, and then we waited some more. The morning broke and wore on, and still we waited. All this time there were more families arriving, all as frightened and confused as we were, some with young children, some with older ones. There were also a few single people.

We children were still scuttling in and out among the legs of our parents, chasing each other, if we weren't crying, which I suppose most of us were. When you are small and young and do not know what is coming next, and mostly all you can see are legs, often the easiest thing to do is to cry. Edit, being as always more alert to what was going on around her than her younger brothers, was helpless with terror, and desperately held on to my mother's hand. I, becoming hungry and ever colder, was wailing mercilessly.

By this time a number of guards had joined the two who had come for us. And they were just as nasty. They barked instructions at the top of their voices; there were vicious thumps, blows and cuffs around the back of the head—either with short whips or heavy gun butts. This carried on for hours, and we were given no more food and no more water. My father, still with a bloody, broken face and broken foot, eventually fainted, and lay on the ground until the frantic ministrations of my mother brought him back to consciousness.

At last we were ordered to move on. We were marched to the railway station, which I think was at the far end of the town. The younger children were trying to keep up, and falling down, while mothers were trying to carry their babies and at the same time to keep control of the other children. There was a great deal of shouting, shoving, pushing and wailing from prisoners and guards alike.

I know, though I am not sure quite how, that some rather elderly professor of something or other had got hold of my father and had begun telling him that things were ever so for the Jews. It was best just to accept what was happening, he said, as another episode of their long history. My father, wretched with guilt and pain, was dragging his broken body through the streets of this town on the way to almost certain death. I can only imagine that he did not find this helpful.

Eventually the miserable rabble arrived at the station. Again we were told to form a line on the platform, and this we did with as much success as in the square. Again, we were beaten and shoved into position.

Our guards were brutal, but this was nothing compared to what was to come. These were local men, for the most part, and probably would have known many of us. A lot of them had joined the Nazi party in the interests of self-preservation rather than for any ideological reason. They were most likely finding it difficult to bash and thump a neighbour, the wife of an acquaintance, or someone they went to school with, with any deal of enthusiasm. This is not to say that they were gentle. They did bash and they did thump, but sheepishly, uncomfortably. They had lived with these prisoners as equals, part of a community. Remembered empathy stayed their whips and forced them to hold back.

It was here that the men were torn away from the women and children. This caused a flood of wailing and misery, as husbands and wives tried desperately to hold on to each other and to their children. Many got separated and then managed to rush back into each other's arms, only to be wrested apart still more brutally.

The children who had been crying, running, laughing and playing, gradually became quiet when we realised that now, something really serious was taking place. Until now our mothers had carried themselves with clenched teeth, tensed muscles and stern faces, making great effort to exert the little influence they could over the situation, calming their children and reassuring their husbands. Now they were weeping, loudly and abjectly, from the pain of separation and the fear of what they would have to face alone.

The guards got louder with their shouting and cursing, and they separated families with some force. They elbowed and jostled the men to one end of the platform, and made the women and children wait at the other. This time the wait was not all that long. A steam engine huffed and puffed into view, pulling a long train of large rectangular cattle trucks. At first the young boys, despite our fear and confusion, were thrilled at the sight of the engine so close. But this changed. Slowly, we realised the renewed dismay of our mothers. They stared at the trucks, silent and aghast.

With what was now the normal shouting, bashing and cursing, we were pulled from the top, pushed from the bottom, and crushed into them.

———•———

The cattle trucks. There has been a lot written about them; there have been pictures taken; there has been much shaking of heads and mutterings of 'how terrible'. This all from the outside. I was on the inside: I experienced what they were really like, and that experience haunts me to this day.

They were huge, with large metal doors and broad wooden slats lining the walls—and people were packed in until the sides heaved and the floor creaked with our weight. There was only a small ventilation hole in one corner, a gap in the slats. The air was becoming short and moist even before the doors were tied shut. Those shrewd enough, or those who had already acquired some of the animal opportunism they would come to depend on for their survival in the camps, tried to elbow and shove their way towards it. But throughout the journey, that part of the truck was the most densely packed, and the one from which the guards would eventually drag the greatest number of corpses.

My mother managed to position us in a corner. She spread her feet and made a pocket of space between her body and the wall, in which we three older children cowered, protected from the worst of the crushing weight of living bodies. She held my baby sister, wrapped in a thin white blanket, in her arms. There was some thin brown soup and water in large pails, which people were handing round. My mother mixed some water in with the soup and fed a little to my baby sister.

The train shunted out of the station and began its journey westward, and we remained like this for the interminable hours during which it chugged on and on across the continent. Mothers took turns holding their young children up to the ventilation hole to let them urinate; those too large or heavy to reach it defecated where they were. The soup had been rancid and many began to vomit. The smell grew steadily stronger; the children and many of the adults were howling incessantly. A large, formidable-looking woman tried to make some order. She was Mrs Hollander; she had come from the same town and my mother knew her well. She arranged that some people should sit, some stand and some lie down, and rearranged them from time to time so that others could try to sleep. But eventually her efforts broke down and the few who managed to sit or stretch themselves out on the floor were trampled.

It must have been six hours before the train hissed to a halt. The guards formed a wide circle around it before releasing the doors of the trucks. People poured out into the siding, and from those few who had managed to contain themselves now came eruptions of vomit and faeces.

I saw one girl who had come out of one of the less crowded trucks moving away from the train, reluctant to urinate among the mass of people. As she moved further from the crowd she was spotted by one of the guards, who fired a shot over her head. The girl panicked, motioned to two others, her sisters or companions, and all three began to run wildly towards a patch of wilderness beyond the siding. The guard, without further warning, drew his rifle and fired a single shot at each of the girls. All three fell motionless into the snow, and were forgotten.

I can remember this incident as clearly as if it had happened yesterday. The colour of the girls' heavy overcoats; the expressionless features of the guard as he drew aim and pulled the trigger those three times. Yet I have no memory whatsoever of my feelings at the time. I was not yet five years old and three young girls had been killed in front of my eyes, but I cannot remember how I felt about it. I have the general sense of being overwhelmed, from the moment we were taken from our home until I found a new home some years later, and perhaps that numbed me to the fear and horror of what I saw.

Perhaps my youth, the very thing that made me so vulnerable, also protected me. I was just too young to understand what was going on, and therefore I was prevented from feeling the full horror of it.

I think it is more likely, though, that I have tried to forget. It has not been a conscious attempt, but a purposeful one nonetheless. When I think of myself on a cattle truck or in a concentration camp, it is always with the impression of being outside myself, looking on. There is a helpless little boy, but is it really me? Even after all these years I have difficulty believing it, and that is crucial, I think, to my having been able to grow up and lead a reasonably normal life. At some point in my life, I dissociated myself from all that pain, and so have been able to survive it.

———•———

After a while we were forced back onto the trucks. There was more beating, more cruelty this time. The uniforms were no longer the dark blue-green of the Slovak guardists, but the grey coats of Hitler's SS, and the behaviour of the guards changed along with the uniforms. There were no more vestiges of empathy. To these men and women we were subhuman—animals—and that is exactly how they treated us.

The interior of the trucks was utterly filthy now, and we thought that being confined in there any longer was more than we could take. But our portion of the train was all women and children—terrified, and no match for the SS guards. There was no way we could make any sort of effective protest—and those who had seen what had happened to the three girls realised the danger of doing so. We were crammed back inside and the doors were tied shut.

This time we did not stop for about 36 hours. There was no more food. The sickness brought on by the last ration wore off slowly, only to be replaced by utter weakness and terrible pangs of hunger. People, lacking the strength to keep themselves upright, began to collapse. They did not get up again. Again, my mother had been able to carve a space for us in a corner, and we were spared the worst of the crushing. I even dozed a little, my young body's need for sleep overcoming the terrible hunger, the stench and the fear. But for my mother, responsible for four young lives and no doubt painfully aware of the utmost degradation, there was no such reprieve.

When we stopped the next time my baby sister was gone. What a word to use: gone. So final. She had barely learned to walk and her life had ended. Had she suffocated, starved, died of sickness? Who knows? I do not even know her name.

The picture of what happened next, like the shooting of those three girls, is still crystal clear in my mind. I am on the cattle truck, looking down on the platform. Edit is behind my left shoulder and Aladar is behind my right. Being the smallest, I don't know how I managed to get to the front, but there I am, still demanding my mother's attention and her hand to help me jump down onto the platform. Mother is already down there, holding on to a tiny bundle, which I know is my baby sister, dead. There is a guard—whether he is Polish, Czech, or German I cannot say, since I do not know what country we are in, never mind what town or station— and he is pulling at the bundle, trying to tear it from my mother's hands. My mother is holding on fiercely, holding on with all her strength. The guard gives it a sudden jerk, and wins the struggle. He takes the bundle in one hand, gives it a cursory inspection, and throws it swiftly over the wall at the back of the station. My mother gazes at him, shocked and powerless, and this bundle with no name, my baby sister, is gone.

And my mind, with 65 years of happenings stored on the hard disk, takes out this memory and keeps it to the front. Why? Does this bother me more deeply than the rest of the chaos and confusion, brutality and murder? It is so long ago that I cannot put a face, never mind a name, on my baby sister. I hardly remember playing with her, or being a little boy, annoying her, pinching her to see if she really was asleep. In reality I hardly remember her at all. But I can still see this bundle in my mother's arms, my mother with the black hair—the corpse of a little girl, thrown over a wall in a station in central Europe in the winter of 1944, because her father was a Jew.

Does this bother me? You bet. This was my little sister, and I wasn't given a chance to know her. Would I have sorted out her boyfriends for her, and kept away the dodgy ones? Would I have asked them what their father did: did he have any land, did he have any stock? When she had a bust-up I might have told her that not all boys were like that one. 'And what do you know about it?' she would have cried, and flounced off in tears. Or would she? I will never know. But yes, I am bothered; I am hurt—immensely so. Someone took my baby sister and threw her over a wall. She was my baby sister. We had a right to know each other, and they took that from us.

But there is nothing I can do, so I have learnt to live with this memory. I know what I can change and what I cannot. Don't they say it is the wise man who can tell the difference between the two? I am not a particularly wise man. But in this I can tell the difference.

—•—

Finally, the train arrived at its destination. As with most of the transports at this stage of the war, a third of the people on it were already dead. They had fallen where they were and were walked on or sat on, and the smell of rotting human flesh compounded the horrific odours already present in the trucks.

This was Ravensbrück.[2] Not one of the bigger camps, but one of the most deadly. For those who do not know, and that is getting to be more and more people, the camps were more or less specific. It is generally agreed that there were around 1,600 of these places scattered throughout Europe. Some of these were holding camps—concentration camps in the proper sense. Some of them were work camps. The inmates of these had the privilege to work for the fatherland until they could work no more. Then they went to the gas chamber— that is, if they did not die from exhaustion or starvation. Some were both work camps and death camps, like Auschwitz-Birkenau[3]—where most prisoners, upon arrival, were lined up, inspected by the camp doctors and divided into two groups. Invariably the larger group was sent directly to be exterminated; those fortunate enough to have been selected were forced to perform backbreaking physical labour.

A handful were out-and-out death camps. People arrived and were murdered. No slave labour, no dying from overwork, no starvation rations. Gas chamber. End of story; end of life. In these there was only one work detail, the *Sonderkommando*—those prisoners forced to empty the gas chambers and fill the crematoria. They rifled the corpses for rings, gold teeth, anything of value, before loading them into the ovens and then removing the ashes. The fate of the *Sonderkommando* was the most horrific, because after a certain time, these people were exterminated themselves—but unlike those who had gone before them, they had no illusions. They could not deceive themselves into believing they were going to take a shower. They knew exactly what was happening.

Ravensbrück had been a labour camp, predominantly for women. But it was now the end of the war. The Nazis, desperately trying to hide what they had done from the advancing Russians, were moving their vast hordes of prisoners west. Now Ravensbrück was being used as a death factory, but also as a staging post between the still-occupied east and the vast camps in the interior of Germany. By the time we arrived, they were slaughtering one portion of the prisoners of Ravensbrück, and moving the other portion on.

When the doors of the trucks were finally opened, the women and children who had survived were sent to the right of the platform. The men went to the left and were marched off—as I now understand, straight to the gas chamber. My father was among them. We never even saw him when we got off the train.

I often think of him, especially when I am in my worm-sucking mode. What must it have been like for him—his wife and children going one way, and he another? Did he know what had happened to his youngest child? I like to imagine not—for his pain, as he went to his death, must have been great enough already. He was Jewish, the cause of all our trouble, and his spirit had not been strong enough to keep to the safety of the woods. Did he think that of himself?

I have a strong sense of family in me, perhaps strangely for one of my history, and I am proud of him. Although he had been degraded and tortured, he tried to hold himself tall and be the head of his family. How many of us, if we were tested in the same way, would show the same fortitude?

And my mother, who would not renounce her man. I am proud of her also. I hope some of those genes have been passed on to me. Would my parents have been proud of their son if they had lived? I hope so. Sixty years after their deaths, of course, it is useless to speculate. But if you have a father and mother like that, mind them. Unless you are like me (who has had three mothers) you don't get any more.

I have little memory of the time we spent at Ravensbrück. We did nothing, other than wait for the next meal, such as it was, look for food, and in general keep out of the way of the guards and the grown-ups. After a short time—a week, perhaps two—we were moved on to the west.

———

This was to be the final stage of our deportation, and the final journey of my mother and my brother.

This time, we were forced onto a small number of buses. We were still together as a family, minus our father and baby sister, and there were also a few of the group that had come from our village, and had been with us since the town hall. Mrs Hollander was still there, along with her daughter and another woman. I think this must have given my mother some kind of solace. For what it was worth, she wasn't completely alone in this ordeal.

The bus was similar to the cattle trucks—just as sordid, smelly and dirty. For some reason I can remember that the headlights were shaded. Again, it was extremely overcrowded; needless to say, there were no seats, and bodies were crushed against each other as before. The children who were left by this time were utterly desolate; for what had started out with an element of adventure, albeit a rather scary one, was now a journey of total misery into the unknown. The mothers were doing the best they could for the very little ones, but the older children had to fend for themselves.

Some of the passengers had been in Ravensbrück and other camps for a long time. Having been there for only a week or two, we were still relatively strong, but those who had come from the labour camps were already on death's door, ravaged by long-term hunger, malnutrition and overwork. People, especially the very old and the very young, began to succumb easily; corpses began to accumulate, and this made it even more difficult to find space enough to breathe. To make room, the dead bodies were shoved unceremoniously into a rough pile at the back of the bus.

There were some who, as well as being weakened, had slowly lost their minds. I can remember an old lady moving towards me, with hooked fingers and long yellow nails outstretched. She had madness in her eyes—pure and utter madness. I think she intended to strangle me, to put me out of my misery. My mother saw her coming and interposed her own form, hiding me behind her skirts. I howled with fear, but luckily the woman was unable to get close enough in the throng.

The roads we were travelling on were not in much of a condition. The Allied Air Force had managed to make a ploughed field out of most of them, so the bus had to weave, wander, wobble and turn all over the place. All this extra motion was making us much more uncomfortable. Anyone who had not been ill, or who was getting better, now got worse again from travel sickness. I was very sick. In fact, for years afterwards I felt unwell on any moving vehicle.

As the journey went on it all became much quieter. We had departed at dusk, the idea probably being that we were safer from Allied bombs in the dark. The night was now black as pitch. There were no more shrieks, no more wailing. Instead, we children set up a kind of collective moaning, which was all we were able to manage.

THE BEGINNING

At one stage we were passing through a large town, maybe even a city—which may, in fact, have been Hamburg. All at once I heard the drone of propeller-driven aeroplanes and then fierce, deafening blasts, incredibly close, it seemed. An Allied air raid. The bus driver, who must have had local knowledge, began to use back roads to get around the city and avoid the bombing, but the blasts kept sounding on both sides. My mother was desperate to protect her children, and did the most practical thing she could to make sure we were not hurt. Carefully, she began to hollow out a hiding place in the pile of corpses at the back of the bus. We climbed in among them and she carefully covered our bodies with the lifeless limbs and torsos until the raid had passed.

The sound of a propeller-driven aeroplane, even now, sends shivers up my back. Thank God there aren't very many left. 50 years on, whenever I hear one, my immediate instinct is to get inside. Get out of the open. Get under the dead bodies. Imagine that—a boy of four and three quarters, hidden under a pile of dead bodies, to stop him from becoming one. Things were now so unreal, so out of any recognisable context, that for my mother, hiding her child under a pile of dead bodies was in fact the right thing to do.

I often think about the adults, the mothers. What could have been going through their minds? As children, we were concerned with having food in our bellies and our protectors by our sides. In time, this is what the adults would be reduced to also, but for now they carried bravely the load of responsibility for their children's safety; they were wracked by the psychological degradation of which we, as children, had no knowledge. Perhaps worst of all, whereas the misery of the children came solely from the present, they must have had some idea of the horror that was to come. And where we children hoped for relief, they must have known that there would be none.

The husbands of many of these women had already been taken. They had, so their families were told, gone away to work, or joined the army. The odd postcard had arrived saying that things were fine and that they would be home soon. But usually, by the time these postcards arrived home, the men had been eliminated.

I wonder whether, trundling across Europe on a squalid bus, surrounded by bodily emissions and decaying flesh, the corpse of her baby daughter having just been wrenched from her arms and flung over a wall, my mother was glad or sorry that she had refused to sign that piece of paper. A few weeks beforehand she had been at home with her family, doing what mothers do. I have said that I do not blame her. I wonder if I do? Do I blame her, deep down? How do we know what is going on in our minds? Normal people, whatever they are, have enough difficulties with their innermost thoughts; how the hell do people like me manage?

Years ago, I met up with a psychiatrist from Israel. He had been in Dachau as a child with his father, who had died there. He seemed to spend a lot of his time wondering if he had done all he could to save his father. I picked him up from Dublin Airport, and throughout the drive he kept asking me questions—which, of course, is what people like him do. Apparently I was not as forthcoming as I might have been, for with a touch of gentle exasperation he asked me, 'Why do you always answer a question with another question?' I, with all sincerity, replied, 'Do I?' At that point, he gave up.

And even now, after many more years of thinking and thoughts, I seem to have more questions than answers—so I will return to the facts.

———————

There were many families like us. From the camps of Poland, Czechoslovakia and eastern Germany, thousands upon thousands were arriving in the west in transports of one kind or another. The Russians were closing in from the east, the British and the Americans from the west. The Nazis, realising that their crimes would now be discovered and would have to be accounted for, made a desperate attempt to hide what they had done. They blew up gas chambers and knocked down crematoria. They burnt documents and destroyed registers. And they emptied the concentration camps in the path of the advancing armies.

The much-vaunted Nazi efficiency was now spiralling in on itself. The Reich was beaten and it was becoming clear that the Final Solution would never be completed. Yet the round-ups of Jews, Slavs, homosexuals, gypsies, disabled and handicapped people, socialists, communists and Jehovah's Witnesses continued relentlessly. The reason for killing by now had disappeared, and the killing machine was breaking down. Yet the killing still went on. Prisoners were now simply packed into concentration camps in the west—not to be gassed or worked to death, but slowly and perhaps still more painfully to be slain by malnutrition, typhus, typhoid and tuberculosis.

60-odd years on, we shall never know what, other than out-and-out evil, drove these people on. But whatever the reason, their hate was so all-consuming that when things were coming to an end, the battle over, the foe victorious, the murder continued.

Good fortune is a relative term. If I have a broken leg and you have a broken finger, then you are more fortunate than me. If you stay in a death camp and I get moved on, then I am more fortunate than you. So relatively speaking, we had been fortunate. We had been transported 200 miles from Ravensbrück in an old bus, crammed to suffocation point and under fire from enemy bombs. Some of us had died but most, for now, had survived.

Of those others who had also, for the time being, escaped being exterminated, thousands were being force-marched towards the west. These were people who had been taken from their homes and separated from their families. They came from all parts of Europe and spoke all the languages of Europe. They had been transported in cattle trucks, as less than cattle. They had been locked up, starved, worked till they were near death, stripped of clothes, hair, all semblance of human dignity and all semblance of humanity.

Now, these thousands—half-naked, half-starved, and some half-crazed—were made to walk for miles across the snow and freezing ground. The death marches.[4]

Many did not make it. If they fell they were either shot where they lay or left to die in the cold. Some people did actually manage to escape by wandering off into the forests—in many cases only to freeze or starve to death. The rest finally arrived, by now more like ragged, wretched scarecrows than human beings, in the camps of the west.

So it was that thousands were dumped in a concentration camp not far from Hanover in northern Germany—the concentration camp of Bergen-Belsen. Like my family, many had left their homes not long beforehand; many others, like Anne Frank, who was to succumb to typhus there in early 1945, were veterans of camps like Auschwitz. Many had been transported in the filthy cattle trucks; some had managed to survive the death marches. But they arrived, inexorably, in their hundreds and in their thousands.

———

Belsen. Perhaps I should start this part by saying what Belsen was not. At the beginning it was not a concentration camp, though at the end of the war it did become one. There was and still is an army barracks in the town, and originally it was a prisoner-of-war camp.

Then Belsen became a detention camp. This was to hold political prisoners, as well as important Jews with rich relatives abroad who were to pay a ransom for their release, and some Jews the Nazis were hoping to exchange for some of their own soldiers captured by the Allies. There was also a German military hospital, which got a fair bit of use when we were liberated.

The conditions at this time were not extreme—but this, like good fortune, was relative. Then, as the camps from the east were being emptied to the west, one Josef Kramer was sent from Auschwitz to take command. Things moved up a gear, and Belsen became a concentration camp with all that term entails.

There was no gas chamber, although there was a small crematorium. The crematorium was not much use in the end—it was far too small to be able to deal with the huge number of bodies that piled up day by day. A camp for women and children was fenced off some way from the main camp, and was very quickly filled.

The prisoners were kept in a series of wooden barracks, each filled with three rows of trestle beds. There was also a very large gallows where, presumably, prisoners were executed—although this was not a feature of my conscious memory until some time after I got to Ireland. One day, I was driving with my new father; I think he was taking me back to boarding school after the holidays. We passed some electricity poles in a field at the side of the road. As I saw them, a shiver went down my spine. He asked me what was wrong, and I replied that for no reason I understood, that I just did not like those poles. 'Not surprising,' he said to me. 'They look just like the gallows in Belsen.' When the British Army got there, he added, there were five or six bodies swinging from them, as had been usual. Whenever I catch sight of one of those poles, I still shudder.

———

When we arrived in Belsen it must have been January 1945. I cannot be sure, and neither can anyone else, because when the SS left they destroyed most of the records. It was late evening, which meant that the 200-mile journey from Ravensbrück must have taken almost 24 hours. Our bus, like the cattle trucks, was rank with excrement, urine and vomit, and piled high with corpses. None of the guards batted an eyelid at the sight: I don't suppose it was any different from all the other transports which were now arriving. There was, I remember, some consternation about the bodies. The problem was not about the fact that these people were dead, but about who was going to do the paperwork. I have a vague idea that the driver was charged with the job, but seemed to have had enough and stormed off like a spoiled child. How strange that such a thing as petulance could exist in these surroundings.

Shortly after we arrived we were made to strip completely. We were herded into one of the huts and lined up in front of one of the men in grey. They made no distinction between the strong ones and the weak, or between the adults and the children and the frail old women. The man was holding a huge fire hose and was pointing it vaguely at the line of people. Someone shouted something in German; the man positioned the hose under his right arm and drew back one of his legs, steadying himself against being propelled backward by the pressure that was about to come. All of a sudden, freezing water began to shoot out of the hose. It hit me with huge force. Its impact on my skin was such that I was rolled around like a piece of tumbleweed. It burned fiercely. I cried out with pain but was unheard above the gushing of the water.

This is another memory I had lost, or repressed, until

recently. I have and always had, I thought, a dread of showers and of swimming. For a long time I thought that I was just a coward when it came to that kind of thing, but Suzi, one of the other children my new father eventually brought to Ireland, was able to remind me about the fire hose. She, too, lived with a phobia of showers and gushing water for 50 years. I should mention that I have never had any problem having a bath, so I don't smell. At least, not a lot.

They made us dress in the uniform of the camp—trousers with thick vertical stripes and a striped garment a bit like a dressing gown—and with the now quite normal beating, yelling and swearing in numerous languages we were driven into one of the barracks.

All the huts in Belsen were the same; indeed, they seem to have been nearly identical in a great number of the camps. They were wooden, and very long. There was only one door, in the middle of an end wall; there were a few windows down each side. I am not sure about the floors, because they were for the most part covered in straw. Some of the older camps, dating from the 30s, would have had some concrete buildings. But when it came to the Final Solution, I suppose, there was no time and no need for the concrete, so they used timber. No doubt these buildings were erected by their future inmates.

Inside our hut were three lines of trestle beds, in bunks three beds high. In Ravensbrück, I think, we had had two beds between the four of us, but here we were crammed into one. It is not really all that difficult to see where I get my fear of crowds. The hut was already oppressively crowded.

I remember that when new prisoners were deposited in our hut there was always much discussion and speculation as to whether they would get the top, middle or bottom bunk. The top one had its problems, and these got worse as the snows eventually melted and the temperature rose. It was swelteringly hot up there and very moist, and the hot air carried the worst of the stench upwards. The air was so foul that it would be almost impossible to sleep, even if pain, hunger and the incessant retching of the sick did not stop you. The middle bunk was not so hot and the stench was not so strong there—but if the people overhead were suffering from diarrhoea, which most of us were, this would fall down on top of you between the bare slats. The bottom one was reasonably cool and the odour was not too bad, but the excrement, vomit, sputum and sometimes blood from both families overhead would fall, constantly, onto your bunk. I have read that towards the end, when they had become too weak to get out of the way, some people actually drowned in their bunks from this.

We were taken to a middle bunk, which is where we stayed for the duration. There was no toilet. I remember noticing the family in one of the bunks in the next row. They had a small child who wanted to pass excrement. They must have been newly arrived, because the mother was looking around in vain for a toilet, or a bucket, or something. In the end she found a thermos flask and held it up to the child's backside.

Shortly, we were given some sort of food. I think it was milk and bread, for some reason not the watery soup of boiled root vegetables that would be our usual fare. After that, the doors were locked and we were left for the night.

———•———

The cat is out, so for once I don't have to share my seat. I am wondering to myself why I feel I have to go on about the bodies, the violence and the squalor. At the beginning I said that there would not be much gore. Now though, I feel that that is such an essential part of my story that to leave it out would only be telling the half of what happened. Yes, I know we have all seen the pictures, read the books, watched the documentaries. But for this to make any sort of sense, I have to make some mention of what the conditions were really like. For it is me, myself, I am writing about. Although I was very young, these sights and these events made me what I have become. So to know me, you must also know some of what I saw.

Over the years, I have been speaking to schools and various other groupings about Belsen. They all have questions and I try to make them understand as best I can what it was actually like. I show them a rather sick-making video and try to answer their questions, however naïve they might be. I remember one instance a few years ago, when I had finished my speech, one young girl with a very earnest look on her face piped up. 'What did you do for education?' she asked me. I had a strong urge to tell her that we had Montessori three times a week and went on nature walks. I am glad to say I thought better of it, just. For what would she have known about such a place as a concentration camp? Another time I was answering questions in a primary school. There was a small girl of about five just in front of me. She had had her hand up for ages and the older ones kept getting in before her. In the end I pointed straight at her and she asked me, 'What did you do for your birthday?'

How do you answer that when you are talking about mass slaughter? So I thought for a while, and then told her that I had not been there for my birthday, but if I had been I was sure there would have been a party. I suppose that having my innocence taken so violently from me had taught me the value of innocence in others. They will grow up soon enough.

What happened over the months I spent in Belsen has no particular order or sequence in my mind. I can remember certain instances very clearly, but I can only guess where they fit into the sequence of time—except for the fact that as the months wore on, things got worse and worse. We were hungry all the time, and washing did not feature as a major priority. There was only one pump for the whole camp: water was very scarce and probably contaminated.

The latrine was always full to overflowing. It was necessary to balance on two pieces of wood which were stretched across the foul-smelling pit while you did what you had to do. I can recall seeing an old man balancing on these planks, squatting over the latrine. A German guard who was watching quite suddenly stepped up to the old man and pushed him off balance with his bayonet. He toppled with a splash into the fetid pit, and I do not remember seeing him come back up. I think the guard did it for fun. At any rate, after he had pushed the old man he walked off nonchalantly, as if he had done nothing more serious than swatting a fly.

Many people, too ill or weak to get to the latrine, urinated and defecated on the floor of the huts or even in their bunks. The general state of the huts was appalling. Everywhere the ground was littered with the bodies of the dead and the dying, and covered in stuff that should have gone elsewhere. Yet, as children, we continued to play and run around for as long as we could—before, inevitably, disease caught up with us.

There were one or two cookhouses around the camp, and a few people were assigned from each hut to collect what food there was. It would come in great big cauldrons, once a day at midday. There was about half a pint per person—just enough to keep us from starving. It never varied—a thin vegetable soup which was probably just turnips and carrots boiled in water. Years later, when I worked as a chef in upmarket hotels and restaurants, my stomach would lurch at the smell of boiling carrots. I still loathe that smell.

Every morning, in the dark, there was a roll call. There is no way that we inmates were going to go anywhere. They had a barbed-wire electrified fence to keep us in. Most of us would have been too weak to get over it, and there were guards with rifles in each of the watchtowers overlooking all parts of the camp. When things were really bad, some of the prisoners would head for the wire—thinking that dying from gunshots or electrocution would surely be more merciful than typhus. It seldom was. The guards would let them get caught on the wire, wait until they were convulsing violently from the jolts of electricity that coursed through their bodies, and then take pot shots at them.

My memory of this, strangely, is that it was a very ordinary thing. I cannot remember being upset about it. Is it my memory again, shielding me from the pain of these recollections? Or could it be that a four-year-old boy could have become so used to seeing people electrocuted and then used for target practice that it did not affect him? It is amazing what people can get used to. After all, the guards themselves had been ordinary men and women, with mothers and fathers, husbands and wives, perhaps even children. They had been hardened by years witnessing the brutal treatment of the prisoners and taking their own part in brutalising them; they had been indoctrinated to believe that the people they were guarding were as worthless as vermin—and so they were able to kill them for fun.

The roll call. The whole camp would be assembled outside in a kind of square or courtyard, and lined up according to which hut we belonged to. We were supposed to stay still and not run around, but the children who still had strength, being children, did what children always do. We scampered around, played games, poked our heads out of the line and made faces at each other. This always made our mothers frantic, because it was a well-known fact of life that if you drew attention to yourself you could, and often did, get the belt of a gun butt on the back of the head.

For a long time I was baffled as to the purpose of these roll calls, since there was no real chance of escape. I thought that it might just have been another method of torture, since we often had to stand for hours in the freezing cold. I thought that perhaps the ingrained Nazi bureaucracy was continuing to generate red tape even though its purpose was obsolete. But eventually, I realised that their primary purpose towards the end was far more pragmatic. We were being counted to see how many had died during the night.

At first, the prisoners had been able to take out the dead in the mornings and leave their bodies around the side of the barracks. A hand cart, pulled and pushed by the inmates, of course, would come and collect these. They were taken to be burnt and then, as the numbers became too much for the little crematorium, they were left in big piles at the side of the huge pits the guards were opening as mass graves. But as we all got weaker and weaker, few had the strength to haul the corpses out of the huts, never mind cart them to the burial sites. So we had a roll call. Then they could do the sums and find out how many of us were now dead—and, I suppose, how many people they still had to feed.

One afternoon, out of the blue, they called a roll call. We all lined up in the usual way in the square in the middle of the huts. This time there was an enormous fire lighting in the middle. They were burning a huge pile of wood—large pieces of timber and the odd chair, I think. It was dry and the wood was burning easily, sending thick bright flames high up into the air. There was a large cast-iron sheet on top of the pile of burning wood. We were all lined up in front of the fire, mothers and children.

After we had been standing for a while we became aware of a group of German guards approaching the crowd. There were four of them, and two behind, and they were dragging a naked man. They took him and threw him on top of this cast-iron sheet. He did not cry out; he hardly moved—but he fried to death before our eyes. At this stage the man would not have been much more than skin and bone. Still, the smell of burning flesh was overpowering.

In Ireland, when we used to go to the blacksmith and watch as he fitted horseshoes, I would feel uncomfortable and could not bring myself to watch. Looking back, I can understand why. The hot iron as it burned into the tissue of the horse's hoof made exactly the same smell.

As our mothers tried to shield us from the sight and turn their own faces away, the guards, who were pacing up and down the lines, struck them with their short whips or the butts of their guns. They wanted us all to watch, to witness every detail of the horrendous scene, so that we would know better than to disobey them. That was what would happen if we misbehaved.

At some stage during the first weeks of my internment I came across one of the series of extraordinary people to whom I owe my survival. This was Luba Tryszynska, the Angel of Belsen. She was—is, for I think she is still alive—a Polish Jew who had been deported to Auschwitz with her husband and young son. Her son was sent directly to the gas chamber, and her husband's fate was even worse. He was made part of the *Sonderkommando*—forced to shovel corpses from the gas chambers into the crematoria, knowing that finally, he too would be gassed to death.

According to legend, Luba escaped being selected for elimination because of her beauty—which was of the earthy, buxom variety—and she managed to maintain something like safety by getting work in Auschwitz as a nurse. She was eventually transferred to Belsen with her inseparable companion, a Slovak girl named Hermina Krantz.

The story goes, and I think it is true, that soon after Luba arrived in Belsen she heard a terrible howling coming from the hut beside ours. She and Hermina went to investigate, and found 54 Dutch orphans inside. Luba was intensely motherly and generous, and besides, she had nothing else to live for. So she took it upon herself to look after them.

Where or how she managed to get the extra rations no one

knows, and no one was brave enough to ask. It was certainly a case of need over moral niceties, though; her looks, which had already saved her life, most probably got her into the favour of the more friendly SS guards. Whatever the means, she managed to procure firewood, bread, coffee, milk and even jam. Some of this, as we wandered around the huts, came our way too. As far as Luba was concerned, we were all children and all in need of her care. She would make sure that we had a wash now and then, and she made us run around to get dry, for of course there were no such things as towels. Hermina tirelessly scrubbed our clothes in the meantime, doing her best to boil out the tics and lice that would spread typhus.

Luba had an ample bosom, which I can still recall as a great place of comfort and safety. She taught us songs to pass the time. She picked up the little ones when they fell, and kissed them better. She gave comfort to the older ones, and settled squabbles with a clip around the ear when it was necessary. And she had great success. Only two of the original number of Dutch orphans died.

One of the surviving orphans was Gerry. We met again in the Netherlands in 1995. He was the driving force in a campaign to get recognition for Luba, from the people of Amsterdam, for what she did in Belsen. One day Gerry, myself, and I think my brother Aladar, went on an expedition to the cookhouse to see what we could see, or rather get.

We got as far as the cookhouse without any problem, and somehow we managed to sneak in the main door. But as soon as we did so, a guard caught sight of us. He let out one almighty bellow, which sent us running like the clappers to our respective huts. Gerry had no mother, but mine was aghast by what we had done, and let Aladar and me know in the way that mothers quite often do. Now that I think about it, Mother was quite fond of the clip around the ear. Remember the trumpet. She told us that the guard must have been having one of his better days. God knows they were scarce enough for any guard. He might have shot us.

So the trip to the cookhouse was a dead loss. But it is the nature of children to push the boundaries of safety, of adventure, of boundaries themselves. For example, if we had been in or near an orchard during peacetime we would have done the same thing, because that is what children do. We would have stolen apples, got caught, and faced the consequences. Instead, we went to the cookhouse in a horror camp, risked getting shot, and faced the consequences of that. There is a certain comfort in that thought—in knowing that even in that hellish place, even amongst all that was so evil, so frightening, we were still just children being children.

I have been very good at saying how bad the German guards were to us, and all the horrific things they did. This is all true, but there was one female guard—the exception to the rule. After the liberation, the world marvelled at how another woman, the incredibly beautiful SS guard Irma Grese,[6] could have a heart so ugly as to have beaten and tortured prisoners in Belsen. Our guard was the opposite. She limped horribly, and even at four and three quarters I could see that she was ugly as sin. But unlike Grese, there was still goodness in her, and she took pity on my family and me. I have no idea as to why she picked us. The liberators would later remark on my lovely eyes and all-encompassing grin. Perhaps it was that. Perhaps she had young brothers or sisters, or sons or daughters about our age. Whatever the reasons were, she took what human feeling the Nazi regime had left her and managed, regularly, to take us into a sectioned-off portion of our hut and give out extra rations. This was done in total secrecy. If word had got around in this hut full of starving, desperate prisoners, there would have been pandemonium. I think some of the food must have been her own rations, for I remember getting some rich, garlicky German sausage on one occasion—something even Luba had not managed to get her hands on.

I am pretty sure that these extra bits and pieces, along with what we got from Luba, were the difference between living and dying. This guard was another of the ones who saved me. I have no doubt in my mind that if she had not taken this risk upon herself, I would not be here. You could say, and perhaps with justification, that a few extra scraps of food going to one family while 12 million are being wiped out are of no consequence in the scheme of things. But believe me, if you happen to be a member of that one family the consequences are stupendous.

I know nothing about her, this ugly guard with the limp, or what happened to her after the war. But from her small acts of kindness I have come to another comforting thought. In the midst of all the various evils we inflict on ourselves and on others, someone will come along with a spark of humanity left in them, courage even. And they will do the right thing.

Towards the end the numbers of new corpses were in the high hundreds every day. Any attempt to move them had been abandoned and they piled up everywhere and decayed. The foul stench of death was in every corner of the camp. The sick lay among them, too weak to move, waiting for death, and their number increased steadily. Typhoid, typhus and tuberculosis were now rampant. The level of disease was such that the guards eventually became afraid to go into the camp itself, never mind into the stricken huts. They barked commands through the openings in the walls, and left the Kapos to keep order.

There was a Kapo in each of the huts—one of the Aryan prisoners who had been put in charge, and who gained extra rations and privileges for keeping some sort of order. To have become a Kapo, a prisoner would have snitched on another, perhaps, or beaten up some old man or woman who had broken a petty rule. The guards would then have accepted him or her as one of themselves—almost.

The Kapos, perhaps to curry favour, were just as brutal as the actual guards. With the appearances of the guards becoming more and more seldom, the Kapos ended up doing a great deal of their dirty work for them. When liberation eventually did come, a lot of scores were settled. Many of the Kapos were beaten or shot; some were quite literally torn apart, limb from limb.

Still the transports arrived and people poured into the camp. In the end this space, less than one mile long and half a mile wide, held 60,000 souls—ten times its capacity. My new father later wrote that it held more suffering than had any spot on earth.

On the whole, the children survived better than the adults. I am pretty sure that many of the mothers gave a large portion of their own food to their children. Also, I think it probably had a lot to do with what was going on in our minds. As children, we were hungry, frightened and sick, but we did not know where we were. We did not know why we were in this hellish place, or that most of us were likely to die here. Our mothers knew the whole horror of the situation. They had lived with the protracted degradation of the Jews by the Nazis; they were burdened with the impossible responsibility of looking after their children; they knew the danger of disease; and worst of all, they were aware in a way that the children were not that their dignity had been taken from them in the most horrific way.

We children had the resilience of inexperience. It would affect most of us dreadfully in later life, but for now, this became normality. We adapted and we dealt with it. For the adults, however, this horror could never be normal, and it destroyed their minds and their bodies. And so, at the time when most of the children were still able to play among the rotting corpses, the adults wasted away, fell victim to disease and died by the thousand.

My mother was the first of my family to become ill. She became feverish, and weakened. Eventually she could no longer move enough to fetch water and food for the rest of us. My sister and Mrs Hollander, who was in the same hut, nursed her, but she was getting weaker by the day.

My brother, too, sickened and became feverish. And eventually—three weeks, maybe a month before the liberation—even I was no longer interested in running around. At this stage, I would later be told, I already had full-blown tuberculosis of the spine, but this would not manifest itself until several months later. It was typhus, typhoid or a combination of both that was making me ill.

Edit was still reasonably strong, and looked after us all with fortitude and diligence well beyond her seven years. Suzi, too, being not yet three and too small to play with the few children who still had strength, would run back and forth, scavenging scraps of food for us and the other sick people in the hut. We all slipped downhill, and by mid-April, were just clinging to life.

What I remember of the 15 April is just one specific incident. The memory has never left me and I hope never will, for it is my last link to my mother.

Edit had trotted off with a jerry can to get water. Three days previously, what guards there still were had gone. They destroyed almost all records as they went, but they also committed one last act of devastating cruelty. They turned off the water supply to the pump. The British Army, when they arrived, found only one tank of water, and there was a corpse floating inside it.

The three of us were together, huddled in a corner of the hut. Aladar and I were wide awake, but my mother was drifting in and out of consciousness, her eyes hollow, her cheeks sunken, her body little more than a bundle of rags. Edit came in, carrying the jerry can. She had managed to find some water. She was steaming back up the hut towards us, but halfway up she tripped on some rags. She fell and the water spilt all over the hut floor. Mrs Hollander got up and began to scold her, but she took no notice. 'It's all right!' she was shouting. 'It's all right! We are free!'

This meant nothing to me. I was dismayed with the water having been spilt and began to cry. What was free? Could you eat it? Could you drink it? But the hut became greatly excited and emptied of people until the only ones left were the dead and the dying.

My mother was awake now, and Edit leaned close to her head and whispered, 'We are free, Mama. Mama, we are free.' My mother, raising her eyes upwards so that Edit could see that in her face was no longer fear but relief, and peace, said, 'Look after the boys, my daughter. Look after Zoltan. Never get separated from Zoltan.' And then, with a sigh, she slipped into death.

I lived through what was arguably one of the most extreme experiences of the last few centuries: death camps, gas chambers, murder, starvation, disease. At less than five years old I witnessed the death of three members of my immediate family, right before my eyes. Yet here I am, one of the few who managed to get through all that. Are we blessed, we few? Are we the chosen ones to carry the torch, keep alive the memory of those times? It would be so easy to think so, that the mere fact of our survival makes us special, worthy of attention—of deference, even. Make way, touch your forelock as you pass by, avert your eyes. Here is the chosen one coming along the road. He is special, he was spared.

Rubbish. I am none of that. I am not special. I am not the chosen one, and I hope I never forget it, because, as I keep saying, all of this is relative. That does not make it any less evil, hurtful, or God forbid, less traumatic. But the Holocaust happened to millions all over Europe; we were not special or marked out in any way except by the Nazis themselves. And we are not special now. In fact, I suppose that some of the sadness and badness of all of this is that very fact—that we had done nothing to be picked out in this way. Yes, ordinary we were and ordinary we still are. Our numbers are getting fewer, but time has a habit of doing that to people, and those of us who are still left around would do well to remember that there is a balance to life. While you might think that probability was weighted against us who survived, we did survive. But we must not and cannot think of ourselves as being anything special—because that was all we did.

The special ones in this story are not those who were saved, but those who did the saving. The liberators. These were young men and women, often some of the finest minds of their countries, who had fought their way across Europe to come to such a place as Belsen. They bravely marched in through a broken fence behind a tank, and found 20,000 rotting corpses. And those still alive, all arms and legs, so thin they might have been sticks, waving at them. A horrible moaning, which was the nearest we could get to cheering. The sounds, the sights, the smells, of 60,000 dead, rotting, sick and dying humans. They must have thought they had died and gone to hell.

If you want to raise your hat, touch your forelock, or make way, do it for these men and women. They came upon this hell and suffered its full impact. For us, especially us children, the paradox was that as conditions worsened, we became less sensitive and less sentient. As the horror increased, it lost its horror. With no more warning than rumour, no more ammunition against this horror than righteous minds, what shock the liberators must have experienced. Yet they stayed, and got to work cleaning up the mess.

I am proud of being a survivor. I am glad that I am still here and able to testify to what happened to me and my family. But I am certainly not a hero. I have done nothing more than bear what was inflicted upon me. The people who came in afterwards put right the wrongs of others, and they are the special ones.

It was the British Army who marched into Belsen that day, 15 April 1945. The International Red Cross and other relief groups would arrive over the next few weeks and the relief effort would begin in earnest.

While they entered the camp, I was desolate, aware only that my mother was dead. My brother was still huddled up against her, delirious from fever, not yet knowing that the ragged shape beside him no longer held any love or protection from all that was going on around us, but was just a thing without life.

Edit was aware, horribly so, of this hideous truth, and she knew what job she had been given. She was the protector now, and alone. She carried the responsibility for her two dying brothers. During the following weeks and years she would bear this weight with incredible strength, and in many ways she still does. We three dying orphans clung to the body of our mother and waited.

After a few hours, a tall straight-backed man came into the hut. He was still unable to control a violent reaction of disgust. Most of his face was covered by a handkerchief, designed to keep out the stench, but even so I could see that his face was white as a sheet. Every so often he would retch dryly; I think he had already vomited the contents of his stomach several times over.

The British man had two SS guards with him, and began to give them orders in broken German. *'Heraus!'* he shouted. 'Get to work!' The guards sullenly began to haul the many dead out of the hut. When they came to our corner they dragged my mother's body by the feet out of the hut and tossed it onto a wooden cart, to be taken and thrown into one of the massive trenches in the ground that were already full of corpses. My sister, my brother and I, weak and miserable as we were, could only look on numbly.

The reaction of those who entered the camp on 15 April was first one of disbelief and uncontrollable revulsion. As they approached the fence they vomited, one after the other. After six years in the battlefields of Europe, they had seen death, they had seen suffering—but they had never seen anything remotely like this.

Then their disgust turned to rage. The SS, even after the British arrived, continued to brutalise the prisoners, and when they did so the British were merciless in their punishment. They beat and spat at the SS guards. They fed them on the rations they had given the prisoners. They forced them to do the dirtiest jobs in the operation. They humiliated them by forcing them to pose for photographs in pits full of bodies. Many of the SS guards contracted typhus, and a large proportion of them eventually died.

By the time most of the bodies had been cleared—bulldozed

into the mass graves—the immense task of healing those who were still alive began. For a while, the liberators were completely overwhelmed. Think of them—all young men and women who had been trained to take life, not save it. Nobody had had any experience of this sort of mass starvation or of epidemics of infectious disease. How should they deal with it?

There were all sorts of ideas as to what would be the most effective way to stop the deaths and treat the diseases. But there were so many people so far into the last stages of typhus and typhoid that the bodies continued to pile up. Between 500 and 1,000 people died per day in the few weeks after the liberation. The Army took the deaths badly, of course, but there was no way they could stop them immediately.

The first thing they did after clearing the bodies was to separate the sick from the relatively well—in fact, those who were certain to die from those who had some slim chance at getting better. The soldiers had no choice. If anyone was to be saved, they had to harden their hearts and leave the irredeemable cases to die.

They took over the Panzer Training Barracks adjacent to the camp, and set up a hospital there, as well as commandeering the nearby German military hospital. Both were low on supplies, but in excellent condition. They also erected large marquees with pallet beds and basic sanitary facilities. Doctors and medical resources began to arrive, and slowly, the huts were evacuated. Over several days, they washed each of the prisoners thoroughly, dusted us with strong pesticide to stave off infection, and moved us into the wards.

Next came the problem of malnutrition. What could they give us to eat that our shrivelled bellies would not reject? When the soldiers first arrived they had given us protein-rich military rations—tins of corned beef and sausages, stew and heavy puddings. Hundreds of people devoured this fare but, after months of living on vegetable water, became extremely ill because of it. Many, in fact, died from their reaction of their intestines to this food.

The soldiers then experimented with different types of food, and found that the type of nourishment a patient needed largely depended on his or her condition. Some of the more recently arrived were still strong enough to handle the soldiers' rations; there were also potatoes and bread, and the weaker patients were given milk. The very weakest were given a dietary supplement the British had developed during a famine in Bengal in 1943. It was a kind of gruel made mostly of sugar and milk. It tasted horribly sweet, and most people refused to take it.

There were some attempts to inject us with amino acids, but this was also rejected. The story goes that while the Belsen crematorium had been in use, the SS had injected petrol into the veins of prisoners about to die, so that their bodies might burn more easily in the crematorium. Most of the prisoners had either seen this or heard about it and understandably had a deathly fear of needles. We screamed and wailed whenever we caught sight of one, and by no means could anyone induce us to be injected.

By a lot of trial and error, after plan B, plan C and probably plan D too, a system was eventually worked out whereby we all got a type of food that could be eaten with a minimum of ill effects, and most of us began to get better.

There were setbacks to the Army's work. A short time before, we had been robbed of all dignity and the trappings of normal society and civilisation. For months we had acted according to the principle of survival at any price, and it took time before we would abandon this. At first, quite naturally, we treated all distributions of food as if they could be our last. We wolfed down every morsel we could lay our hands on, despite the consequences for our sensitive innards. Anything we could not eat we hid away—under pillows, inside rags and in other secret places, in case others would steal it. In fact, many of us did that for years afterwards. Much of the distribution of the food was done by the strongest of the prisoners, and those who had been doctors or nurses before their deportation. But they often kept it for themselves or gave it to those who had the strength to fight for it most fiercely. I think one of the hardest things for the liberators was to see this base behaviour, this wild grappling for advantage. These were people whose liberal British education had taught them about the nobility of the human mind, its reason and basic charity. And here they were, faced with the reality that given such circumstances as we were in, the human mind does not stay noble for very long. It was not pretty, and not easy for these men to understand.

Later, nationality began to play a part. If there was any food left prisoners passed it on, but to their own people if they could; in the hospital the nurses would attend first to patients of their own nationality. The Poles did not like the Hungarians, who did not have much time for the Dutch, who hated the Slovaks, and so on. And then there were further divisions along family lines. It was not easy for anyone.

Aladar and I were borderline cases, and were put with those who had a chance of surviving but who were nonetheless very ill. Edit was a little stronger and sent to the well ward—'well' being another of those relative terms I must use to describe the situation. She came to visit us from time to time, and was very anxious to do so, already feeling the responsibility of the task our mother had given her.

And all this time, people continued to die around us. I am inclined to wonder whether for some of them, their physical condition was only half the story. Perhaps enough was enough. Had they seen too much, experienced too much, to go on living? No one can say, but I believe that there is some truth in that. For at the time of the liberation, Aladar, my brother, was in better physical condition than I was. He had the same fever, the same weakness, but where my spine was infected with tuberculosis, he was free of that disease. I began to recover from typhoid or typhus or both, but Aladar got worse. Perhaps whatever it is you are born with that enables you to survive, I had more of. While that quality in me kicked in and I fought to get better, Aladar turned his face to the wall and he died. For him, what he had seen of the world in his five and a half years convinced him that it was not worth living. Why I was not affected in the same way, I do not know. Two little boys, each with the same experience. One lives, one dies.

———

At the beginning of May the International Red Cross arrived, and from that time onward things began to improve immensely. The Red Cross were in a much better position to provide continuing relief than the Army had been. No one foresaw such a dire and extreme emergency, but the Red Cross had been trained for events of a similar nature. After they got there the daily death rate fell and eventually levelled; people began to get better, not only physically, but mentally. Slowly, we began to think of ourselves as people again, to regain our sense of dignity and self-esteem.

Altogether, there were about 500 remaining children. Little by little, most of us began to get back the colour in our cheeks and the twinkle in our eyes. Such is the nature of children that when they get a full belly, shelter and freedom from fear, they very quickly become children again. This is what happened in those army tents. As the Army cleared the camp and the Red Cross began to impose order and structure in the makeshift hospital, we children blossomed. I am told that it was nearly possible to see the bellies become convex rather than concave, and the smiles, fun and laughter return.

As soon as we were able, we would run in and out under the flaps of the tents and around, over and between the guy ropes that were holding them up. I remember one instance quite clearly, where too many of us were running around the same rope. Someone fell, another fell on top and the rope was caught and pulled, hard. The whole tent collapsed on top of the patients and ministering nurses. We got a serious talking to that day, but by and large the young soldiers were so amazed and delighted to see this sudden change in our condition that they did not have it in them to try to curb our enthusiasm. I am quite sure that they themselves took an active part in our games. What the officers thought of all this, as far as I know, is not recorded anywhere.

Eventually, they took a flame thrower to the wooden huts that had been prison, slaughterhouse and mortuary to us for all those months. They burnt them because the fleas, lice and infested filth that were inside would be impossible to remove; but for the former prisoners of Belsen this was a ritual, a cleansing by fire. As they burnt the last hut there was passionate cheering, and that night there was a fervent celebration.

The Red Cross teams were mainly made up of British personnel, though the odd foreigner had also managed to slip in. Among these slip-ins were an Irish paediatrician, Dr Bob Collis, and one of his nurses, Johanna Hogerzeil, whom everyone knew as Han.

It was Han who found me in one of the tents. As soon as she saw me she smiled delightedly. 'Ah!' she exclaimed. 'What an enchanting scrap of humanity! Just one big grin.' Like many people, she took a real shine to me. I am told that I had captivating eyes, a lovely head of thick black hair and a dazzling smile, which drew people to me. People rained attention upon me, and I played up to it. In fact, I believe that that is a large part of the reason why I was able to recover so well from the experience of Belsen. So many survivors became introverted and closed themselves up to the outside. They became unable to express themselves, and therefore lonely. I, on the other hand, was drawn out by much attention and kindness, and was able to be happy. Perhaps if I had been ugly as sin, cross-eyed, with a bald patch, I would have turned out a lot less content. Now my eyes have cataracts, the smile has gone a bit gummy, the hair has for the most part gone, and what is left is rapidly going grey—and people are not as nice to me as they once were. But I can still get through to them, I hope, and for that I am thankful.

Han was the nurse and translator for Bob Collis, the doctor who would take charge of my case and have such a great effect on my life as a whole. Before I saw him for the first time I heard his voice coming down the corridor. He was flanked by all his flunkeys, who all seemed to be hanging on his every word. I didn't understand any English but I remember that he sounded strong. Han, who already knew about me and my sister, told him a little bit about us. He picked me up, prodded me with metal instruments, and gave me small white pills to swallow. I must have liked him, and I immediately trusted him completely—extraordinarily, considering what I had just come through.

I had a habit, I am told, of making strange and unexpected statements. I rather think it was a way of manipulating the adults around me. Sometimes I would make them laugh, but other times they would just be confused. When Han had come across me first I had announced to her matter-of-factly, 'My brother did not eat and therefore he died.'

Now, when the Doctor picked me up for a second time, I had decided. I said to him in German, 'My father is dead. You are now my father.'

Bob spoke only a little German, and Han jumped in quickly to translate. She was careful to tell him what I had said without smiling and without emotion in her voice, so as not to inform his reaction in any way.

The Doctor said nothing but, 'Right.' But at that moment, something happened. I do not know what it was or why it happened, and we were never to discuss it. But a bond was created between the Doctor and me that was to last some 30 years until his death.

———•———

As we gradually regained our humanity, we began to interact socially with each other and with the relief personnel. Of course, many people would still die, and many lives had been irreparably broken. Some, including myself, would never fully recover from the physical damage that had been inflicted upon us; others would never recover from the mental horrors they had endured. But most of those who were sick were getting better, and those who were well were looking forward to going home. The whole place became optimistic, cheerful, even lively. Belsen the horror camp became Belsen the holiday camp.

The Army began to stage elaborate recreational events. Laurence Olivier arrived one day with the Old Vic theatre company and played G.B. Shaw's *Arms and the Man*. There was even a gala day during which the horses that had belonged to the Hungarian guards were commandeered and raced up and down the open parade ground, and there was a huge party and a dance. Far from the fear and suffering of just a few months before, an atmosphere of humour, good-natured sexuality and general friendliness prevailed in Belsen.

Luba had never been too badly affected by illness, and by now was almost completely well. She began to occupy the camp with complete liberty—in fact, with something like dominion. Having been able to bend Hitler's SS to her will, the liberators were a piece of cake. She could, and did, do as she pleased. She and Hermina became the darlings of the soldiers and doctors, and their quarters were one of the epicentres of the social scene.

But still Luba looked after the children, and took complete charge of the Dutch orphans and assorted hangers-on like me. Any child, in fact, who didn't seem to have anyone else to take care of him or her, came under her influence and care. As before, she fed us (again she managed to get extra rations from somewhere), made sure we washed, and even taught us, in a variety of languages—which, despite her lack of education, she had picked up during her time in Auschwitz and Belsen.

Even the doctors and nurses acknowledged her authority where we were concerned. If any of them wanted to see these children, they had to see Luba first. If the children were getting out of line, Luba was called. If any of them was sick, would not eat, bullied the little ones, Luba was called. She was a granny, a mother, a sister. It is fair to say that her young charges improved beyond any others in the camp. It was not just the extra food or the enforced cleanliness. She fulfilled a need in us for something we had lost. She laughed and taught us to do the same, she scolded, she hugged when we fell, she kissed us better, she gave a clip around the ear when we deserved it—and, although I do not wish to be mawkish, I must say that she gave us love. We were not aware of this love as such, and did not think about, but it was something that had been taken away from us in one way or another.

Luba herself thrived on being able to provide this motherly care, but also on the fact that here in the displaced persons' camp, as it was now designated, she was appreciated. When a Dutchman arrived in Belsen with orders from the Queen of Holland for the orphans to be repatriated, Luba was asked to go with them. She did—but in three days she was back in Belsen. The Dutch, she announced to Han, had not given her the respect she was used to. The whole thing was so badly organised she just couldn't believe it. There hadn't even been any beds for the children, and they expected her to stay there? Well, they had another thing coming. If she wasn't valued in Holland, she would go somewhere she would be valued. And with that she marched off to her quarters to resume her reign.

That was Luba. I met her again when she was being honoured for what she did for the orphans of Belsen, after Gerry's campaign. It was the 50th anniversary of the liberation, and there were 36 remaining children, plus husbands, wives and assorted offspring. Han came with me, for she was Dutch and had also taken a large part in the care of the orphans. When I met Luba I thanked her from the bottom of my heart—not only for keeping us alive, but for teaching us to be kids again.

As far as I know, she is still alive and living in Florida with her second husband. The story goes that some time after she lost her first husband in Auschwitz, she met the second one there. He, too, eventually ended up in Belsen, and they fell in love. I don't know whether that is true or not, but it makes a great story. At any rate, the times were so unreal that it is quite possible that that did happen. The last I heard was that he was quite ill and Luba, ever the minder, was nursing him.

Luba, as I have said, was one of the extraordinary people to whom I owe my survival. Two others I have mentioned, and it is they—Bob Collis and Han Hogerzeil—who deserve most of the credit, the acknowledgement and the thanks for my being alive. Of my father, my mother, and my brother, I was not able to say very much because I knew very little. This I am ashamed of and angry about. I wish I had got to know them in my maturity and theirs. I ought to have been able to set down their history, to tell something of the home they lived in and the work they did, so that people might know what kind of people they were. But that was taken away from me. All I was left with were long-forgotten testimonies and the scant facts of my memory, which perhaps speak to some extent for my family, but no doubt are nothing like what they deserved.

On the other hand, I had the good fortune to know Bob Collis and Han Hogerzeil, my personal angels of Belsen, very well. And thankfully, I am able to express more fully what they were about.

Bob, or William Robert Fitzgerald Collis to be precise, was a children's doctor of serious renown. He was Irish, and came from a long line of doctors and solicitors of the Protestant Anglo-Irish ascendancy. His family owned half of the beautiful

Killiney Hill, just south of Dublin, and were mostly assorted surgeons to the Meath Hospital in Dublin. Their busts and portraits still look down imposingly over the corridors and boardrooms there. Bob inherited a lot of money from his father, who had been a miser, terrified of going broke, and sure that his sons were going to break him.

He followed the traditional route of his class from public school in England to Cambridge, then did a stint in Yale, and continued his medical education in London. Like many of the so-called gentry, he had a much greater feeling for his country than a lot of his Celtic neighbours, and he returned to Ireland to set up shop as a paediatrician.

At that time paediatrics was more or less an unheard-of speciality, and Bob did a great deal to bring it to the forefront of Irish medicine in a very short time. In the course of his work, he got involved in the slum clearances of Dublin. The Dublin slums were a very major site of social and medical injustice at that time and Bob, being what he was, got stuck in. This was to the great consternation of his peers, who were still in the age of leaving well enough alone—especially as regards social divisions.

It was in the midst of this work that he met the famous Christy Brown, with whom he became very close friends. Bob's other great passion, apart from medicine, was writing. He moved in Dublin literary circles, and counted important writers like Cecil Day Lewis and Patrick Kavanagh among his friends. During his life Bob would write several prose works, including a book giving an account of his time in Belsen. It was Bob who encouraged Christy Brown with his own attempts at writing an autobiography, which would later be published as *My Left Foot*. Christy, having had little formal education, was unsure of himself and erratic in his writing style. Bob tutored him in the techniques of prose and did a lot to build his confidence. He edited Christy's manuscript and even introduced him to his own agent and publishers.

Bob was also an athletic man, and a great believer in the benefits of fresh air and exercise—as I was to find out growing up. He played rugby, even managing a few caps for Ireland. He owned and rode horses, especially in drag hunts. He was largely uninterested in blood sports, but wasn't above stifling his conscience if it meant a good day's riding with one of the better foxhound packs. Often, such an opportunity would present itself when, for example, a child of a wealthy family needed attention. Have a look at my daughter, then have a good day's sport. Of course, it was very civilised, and nothing so vulgar as money would ever change hands on these occasions.

This was Bob. He was a thoroughbred of the upper crust, a friend of the movers and shakers, but a man with a conscience. You could love him or hate him, which people did in equal numbers, but you could not ignore him.

Of Han, I can tell you somewhat less. I never got to know her that well in my adulthood, but she was also someone who was impossible to ignore.

Han was from Arnhem in the Netherlands. Her ancestors were more or less similar in occupation to Bob's—the family had provided the local doctors and solicitors for generations. They, too, were nobles with a noble conscience. Throughout the war, they risked their own lives to provide a safe house for Jews. Han told me once how they hid a radio wrapped in oilskin in a cesspool at the bottom of their garden so they could listen to BBC broadcasts. This, of course, was a highly dangerous thing to do—but Han, I think, was not averse to a bit of danger.

Han was intensely strong-willed and had very little time for authority. As a result, she managed to get thrown out of most of the schools she was sent to. But she was determined and extremely honourable, and generally went in a straight line towards anything that needed to be done, and did it. She was also very clever, and eventually took a double doctorate in law and medicine.

When the Red Cross team went to Belsen, Han was a student of law. Bob and his team had been sent initially to the Netherlands to deal with the typhoid situation there, and Han had joined him as a volunteer nurse and translator. Having been told that the Dutch situation was under control, it was suggested to them that they should keep going towards the east behind the advancing armies. The concentration camps were being discovered in alarming numbers, and the armies still had fighting to do, so they needed all the help they could get. Bob and Han, with the happy band of

Red Crossers, travelled east, came across the horror that was Belsen, and set about cleaning it up.

While he lived in London, Bob had married, and already had two young sons back in Ireland. But in Belsen, he and Han became lovers. This was not surprising to many people. In such circumstances the need for emotional and physical comfort must have been great, and many took it wherever they could find it. It must have been easy to despair of love, of kindness and of any of the finer human feelings. In my opinion, to have someone with whom to share those feelings would have been a necessity—if only to prove that they existed. Besides, Han was a strikingly attractive young woman, and Bob was a powerful, dashing, rugby-playing doctor.

There is no way I am going to say that their affair was wrong, even if it was. Anyway, I feel that in part it was their feeling for me that brought them together, and perhaps kept them together. The bond between Bob and me affected and included Han. This is not over-dramatic. This is real, the truth—an unexplained and even an unexplainable thing, which under special circumstances can connect people with each other.

Of course, I say all this looking back on what happened. At the time I was completely unaware of their relationship. The age of my innocence was in some ways short but, thankfully, not in others.

Bob and Han must have been genuinely in love, because their relationship lasted. They would continue their affair for years. After Belsen, Bob came back to his wife, Phyllis, in Ireland, but every so often would disappear to London or some other out-of-reach place for a weekend meeting, a medical conference, or to visit an old friend, and would find himself in Han's arms once more. Han worked during much of this time in the Jewish Hospital in the East End of London. She told me once that she loved that job—that she hadn't had as much fun since she left Belsen. When she said that I thought she had gone mad, but what she really meant was the Jewish attitude to life, the humour, the coping mechanisms developed over the millennia. I like to think that I have inherited some of those things.

In due course Phyllis would divorce Bob, he would marry Han and she would become my third mother. But I will explain all that later. What I will also explain is how these two very strong-minded characters managed to get on. In some ways they were very alike. They both had a great sense of justice and injustice, and were never afraid to express an opinion, right or wrong. To the dismay of their contemporaries, they were usually right. It made for some interesting times.

———◆———

As all, or most, of us improved in health, arrangements were made to send us back where we had come from, or as near to where we had come from as could be established. This was a lot more difficult than it sounds, because, of course, the SS had destroyed the records. Most of the younger orphans could only say they came from 'home', and had to be placed according to their language and appearance.

Gypsy children, of whom there had been rather a lot, seemed just to disappear. These children were, according to Bob, the least affected of all the Belsen groups. Their lifestyle meant that they were more used than the others to moving around, and to having to deal with new situations and make the best of them. I remember one young lad, scarcely older than myself, who had certainly been able to keep his wits through all the disorder. He stole a shiny new mouth organ one of the nurses had given me, and quickly vanished from the camp.

The Russian children, of whom there were also very many, were removed very efficiently in large lorries with pictures of Stalin on them. They were not very keen on going back to Mother Russia, and made a great fuss about it.

In fact, there were many of the former prisoners of Belsen who grew attached to the place and were quite resistant to the idea of going home. Here was food, shelter and society, in which many—like Luba—had carved out a sure and comfortable niche of their own. And like Luba, for many more there was nothing left at home but uncertainty. These people would face an arduous journey to their native places, often to find that their houses had been taken over in their absence by their envious (and mostly Gentile) neighbours. Often, they were the only survivors among their family and friends, and would have to face the future entirely alone.

Belsen, on the other hand, had become a place of certainty—something we all needed—and quite a few people actually stayed on until the 1950s. By this time they had a whole community of their own, with a school, a synagogue and anything else that was necessary. Finally, the people who were left in Belsen travelled to Israel, which was the closest thing they had to a home, and settled there.

In the end, there were five orphans who had no one to claim them and nowhere else to go—myself, Edit, Suzi and her brother Terry, and a little German orphan, Evelyn. Bob decided that the best thing to do with us was to take us back to Ireland, in the hope of having us adopted into Jewish families there.

Ever since the day I had called him my father, he had become more and more attached to me, and I to him. He was very fond of Edit too. She had become very silent, and very withdrawn, and I think part of his affection for her was medical. He was eager to witness her recovery, to observe her as she recovered the spring in her step. In the end, he decided that he would not look for a home for the two of us. I had said that he was now my father, and so he would be. He would adopt Edit and me into his own family.

The Swedish Red Cross said that they would accommodate any sick people still too ill to go home while they recuperated, as well as the orphaned children who had no family left, or had not yet been claimed by their relations. I think the numbers were larger than they thought, but they kept their word. The five of us were in reasonable health after several months of good food and attention, but it was decided that some more rest and more attention before beginning our new lives in Ireland would do us the world of good. With a great deal of excitement, tears, laughter and frazzled nerves, we got on a train from Belsen to Lübeck, and from there boarded a shining white ship to Sweden.

On the boat most of us were rather subdued, and I was indulging my bad temper to the best of my ability—which, even then, was formidable. Naturally enough, we had mixed feelings about leaving Belsen. It was the site of the most intense suffering we had ever seen or would again. But it had nevertheless become our home, and we had found love there despite the rest. I seem to remember being brought outside and put on deck, but even that did not shut me up.

Sweden itself, when we got there, was quite a shock to the system. Everything was white, clean and orderly. We were all put into a large house, with a long concrete path leading up to the front door. It was dead straight. There were red and yellow tulips along its borders, all equal in height, evenly spaced, and straight. I wouldn't be surprised if the nurses polished them every morning before breakfast. At the top of the path the girls went one way and the boys went another. There was a heavy-duty washing area, which was constantly full of steam. You went in one end and, as Bob said, came out the other cleaner than you had ever been before.

This was all very different from what we had been used to, and the Swedes were not so indulgent to children as the Red Cross personnel had been. Probably most difficult, though, was the fact that these frosty doctors and nurses actually expected us to behave. We had got away with all sorts of bad behaviour in the Belsen hospital, and it was not at all easy to adjust to the fact that our new guardians would not stand for any nonsense.

In the autumn Bob and Han returned to Germany to witness the trial of Josef Kramer,[7] commandant of Belsen, SS Irma Grese,[8] and other members of the Nazi administration who were responsible for implementing Hitler's horrific Final Solution. This was the first time that they heard the whole story and found out the true extent of Nazi horror, and right then they began their own account of the liberation. Bob and Han wrote a book in which Bob described how he was appalled that such positive evil had been allowed to obliterate decent values. It sickened him that Kramer and his comrades had accepted this evil totally—and still did. It did not occur to them that the systematic destruction of a whole race was at all immoral. Among these people, Bob and Han felt like pilgrims, trying to follow a moral path obscured everywhere by the encroaching wilderness. They called their book *Straight On*.

After the trial, Han went to work for the UN Commission for Refugees in New York, Geneva, the Netherlands and all sorts of other places, and Bob returned to Ireland.

My impression of this time is that every need was catered for, with one rather obvious exception—the kisses and cuddles and hugs we had grown accustomed to. Han was gone, Bob was gone, Luba had gone back to her beloved friend Hermina in Belsen, and we were left with these well-meaning but rather sterile Swedes. I do not mean to be unkind, and of all people I know the dangers of racial stereotypes, but this is what I found there: efficiency, organisation and order in spades—but not too much love. Bob and Han, our newfound security, had dumped us with lots of promises to come back. But we had been there before, and most of us were not yet well enough recovered from the concentration camp to have regained the blind trust in adults that we once had. In the end, as children ever do, we adapted to this new home, and were soon misbehaving happily.

—■—■—

During this time, Bob received a letter. It was peppered with postmarks, and the address read simply, 'Doctor Collis, Ireland.' By all accounts it had called at quite a few ports.

It was from my grandmother. One of the former prisoners of Belsen came from our area of Slovakia and had returned home. He, or she, for I have no idea who it was, had been able to find my grandmother and tell her about the Irish doctor who had done all this work for the children, and that he was bringing some of them back to Ireland. I don't know how she managed it, but Granny was able to get in touch with the Red Cross, who of course traced Bob and forwarded him the letter. Europe was still in turmoil, there were displaced persons all over the place, the communists were coming and everybody was getting ready to start fighting all over again. And this little old lady in a corner of Slovakia was able to find a doctor on the edge of the continent. If I was a dramatic kind of person, I could call it fate. Was it? I wish I knew, for that might sort out quite a few things in my life.

At this point, the Russians had got to Czechoslovakia. Bob always seemed to know someone who would be of use to him. It happened that he had spent a night hidden in an air-raid shelter in London with the then Prime Minister of Czechoslovakia. This man, as Bob told it, was ahead of his time. Perhaps that is why he and Bob got on like a house on fire. Some years later, the communists would get rid of him. He would slip, or fall, or be pushed. But Bob got in touch with him, and he arranged Bob's passage to the Tatra.

So off Bob went, and found my granny, as well as quite a few former prisoners of Belsen who had come from near and far when they had heard that the Irish doctor was coming. I do not know what had happened to the aunts and uncles, but now my grandmother was alone, on a smallholding, and almost destitute.

Bob told her what he could about us, and she in turn told him all about our background. It was this testimony, which Bob recorded in another book, that gave me a picture of my childhood in Slovakia. I can remember only small and specific things, but I can at least imagine the rest. I wonder if she knew about my trumpet, and the clip around the ear I got for filling it with water.

She asked Bob to keep the two of us, to bring us up with him in Ireland. She was a poor old woman, she explained to him. We were young children, and there was just nothing she could give us.

This threw Bob a bit. It was not what he had expected, and I think he saw it as unworthy, as a rejection. Do I feel rejected? Not one bit. Our grandmother was doing what was best for Edit and me as she saw it—and it could not have been easy for her. She had lost her daughter, her son-in-law, and two grandchildren, and she was giving the other two away. I wonder, at times, is this where my mother got her strength, and in turn her daughter, my sister?

Bob stayed there for a few days. There was much feasting and breaking of bread—figuratively, of course, because physically, there wouldn't have been much to feast on. Bob was feted as a hero, which of course he was, and which he knew he was. But that was one of the great things about Bob. He could accept accolades like that in a very gracious manner. I suppose he was used to it.

Granny gave him a few bits and pieces for Edit—they must have been family heirlooms—and Bob got back into his government car and set off back to the other end of Europe. To Edit and myself he never talked much about that visit. He had the idea that we might get unsettled if we had too much contact with our past, but I think it had more to do with the fact that it had quite unsettled him—the welcome he got, the adulation, and the pain and loss of this poor old woman so readily poured forth to him. Underneath the hero-sized ego there was a sensitive man who felt the pain of others, perhaps more than he should. If you had said that to him, you would have got a pretty cutting reply. But that, thank God, was Bob.

Soon, Bob and Han came back to Sweden, and what had slowly become wild now became almost out of control. Poor Swedes. Gradually, I had become very ill again, and probably was not taking my rightful part in the bad behaviour. I was very weak; I was coughing and spluttering constantly and quite painfully. Nonetheless, I can remember the excitement coursing through the place when the news got out that they were back. There was laughing and crying, shrieks and murmurs: 'They've come back!', 'I told you so!', 'I knew they would!' And this was not just from the children. Even some of the Swedes let their guard down and indulged in a bit of emotion. I bet it was good for them.

I had to stay in bed, and was shaking with excitement like a greyhound in the traps waiting for the hare. Then, all at once, Bob and Han bustled in. Immediately, so Han told me, my grin came back, my eyes sparkled, and we were all back to where we had come from. I still recall that moment: it was good.

I stretched my arms out to be lifted and winced, painfully. Everyone was so caught up in being together again that I do not think anyone noticed. But Bob picked me up, and I rubbed my smooth chin against his hairy one. His expression changed at once—from one of gaiety and gladness to one of grave concern. He had his hand on my back, and could feel a large, hard bump.

Bob was a paediatrician, and he knew at once what it would be, but we went through the motions of diagnosis. They took an x-ray, which confirmed what he knew. Sure enough, I had tuberculosis. In the spine.

Bob and Han looked at each other in silence for a moment or two. This complicated things. Bob was to take me with him back to Ireland, to become my new father. A small half-starved Slovak boy was one thing—but one with TB of the spine, for which there was no cure at the time, was quite another.

But then there was Edit. Could she be separated from her brother, whom their mother had asked her to look after just before she died? And if not, what would happen to her? Would she get the stability and love she needed?

Also, there were the other three—Terry, Suzi and Evelyn. The children had been together all this time, for better and for worse. They came as a package. Surely it would be wrong to split them up now, just because of a little bit of TB?

We children were all around, and looked at each other with some bewilderment. We sensed something was not good. We had seen this look in grown-ups before.

Han knew what Bob was thinking. 'You promised,' she said to him quietly. Bob looked at me, hesitated only for a second, and replied, 'Yes. Yes, I did.'

With those words, the tension disappeared from everyone, and the laughing and crying started up again.

Bob, my newfound father. Did he have any idea what he had taken on? I am sure he was only aware, as I was, of what had come about between us. I have no idea what it could be called. A bond? Something. We never said anything much to each other in words, even when I learned English, and we never spoke of it, but this bond, this something was always there.

This bump on my back was the cause of much concern to everyone. TB in the vertebrae is a disastrous thing to have. Assuming you get over the infection itself, there is the almost certain deformity which results from it. It greatly reduces lung capacity, and there is also a chance of loss of mobility should the vertebrae collapse, as they are eaten away by infection. All the time I had been recovering from the awful state my body was in, all the time I had been regaining my strength and my vigour, the disease had been swelling and blossoming in my spine, and now threatened to kill me.

The first thing to be done was to immobilise me so that no damage would occur to the spinal cord, which goes through the vertebrae. This was done by placing my entire torso in a plaster frame. I have no doubt that I howled as they put me into that frame. As you will have noticed by now, I never missed an opportunity to howl. I remember being very alarmed at the idea that I wouldn't be able to run around and play—which was, in fact, a great hardship for me during the following few years. I can also remember wondering how I would manage my bodily functions from withing this contraption. A discussion about this took place between Edit and myself, and she assured me that a hole of suitable size had been left underneath for that very purpose. I reserved judgement, refusing to believe her until such time as the functions functioned—but lo and behold, there was a hole, and it worked just as it was meant to.

As all the children in Sweden got better, grandparents, great aunts, cousins and uncles arrived back to claim them. The house emptied, Bob's work was done, and the time came for us, too, to leave Sweden for Ireland.

One of the Swedish nurses was picked out to come with us—for her nursing capabilities but also for her looks. All we had was a piece of paper with our names on it. Bob was such a big wheel in London and an even bigger wheel in Ireland that he thought legal requirements did not apply to him. But just in case, he made it clear to the nurse that should anybody get too official, it would be quite in order for her to blink, blush, be bashful, and even shed a tear or two. The nurse, God bless her, agreed to do all these things as and if necessary. As we say in Ireland, there was a pair of them in it.

The flight was from Sweden to Northolt, as it was at the time, and from there to Dublin. The English were not too fussy about us, as we were moving on, and let us go without many awkward questions.

The flight this far had been fine. We had not had to go too high, and to the dismay of all, I had found out that with enough wriggling I was able to make my plaster frame roll on the floor. Suzi scolded me in Hungarian, but I was having fun and paid no attention.

During the flight onward towards Collinstown, however, the plane had to fly a lot higher in order to get over the Welsh mountains. This was not too good for me. In fact, it was awful. The higher the plane went, the less oxygen I got, stretched out on my frame. Suzi, who was minding me as usual, called out to the nurse to have a look at me. I had gone a sort of greenish white, with a touch of blue around the nose and mouth. The nurse came and quite possibly went the same colour as I was. She then called the air stewardess, who had a look at the two of us and went into conference with the pilot. Everyone agreed that the plane would have to complete the trip at a lower altitude. Instead of going over the Welsh mountains, we would now go around them. This made the journey much longer, but it worked a treat. The plane came down to a lower altitude, my colour came back to nearly-normal, and my breathing also improved.

In due course we arrived. While I had perked up considerably, the others were now turning the shade of colour I had just lost. It seems that with the lower altitude there was quite a lot of turbulence, which didn't mix with some of the many treats we had been fed upon leaving Sweden. The others were very airsick.

Ireland was a strange country in those days. There had never been a Second World War, rather an 'emergency', and neutrality in theory if not in fact—even if we did extend condolences to the German people on the death of Hitler. The country's bureaucracy was extremely fussy, and there was a lot of unnecessary interest from the civil servants in charge of immigration. But the story of the camps was now familiar even here. Bob explained who we were and more importantly, who he was. Our Swedish nurse waved her chit of paper, blushed and smiled again, and then quivered her lip and threatened to burst into tears. The authorities didn't stand a chance. They looked the other way while we passed through the gates and into the country.

There was a press photo taken at the airport which is now called the 'Belsen children photo'. Like us, it is taken out every ten years or so, digitally enhanced rather than dusted and polished, and put on display. In some ways it is an unfortunate photo. The other children look very pale and wobbly, as if they could throw up at any time, and it looks as if Bob is resting his arm on Edit's head. But there it is; it cannot be changed now. How strange that what history records so often misses the truth completely.

On the other hand, it is all right for me. I am the contented-looking bundle in the plaster cast being carried by two rather attractive young women.

PART TWO

———◆———

THE MIDDLE

. . . and our bodies also
Heavy with weeping, and winds from sternward
Bore us out onward with bellying canvas

—Ezra Pound, *The Cantos*

BACK IN THE LATE 1930s BOB had written a play called *Marrowbone Lane*, inspired by his work in the overcrowded Dublin slums. In it, a country girl comes to the big city, falls for a boy from the tenements, and from there it is all downhill. The play was produced in the Gate Theatre, with some of the foremost Irish actors of the time in the lead roles. As it happened, the female lead was played by Sheila Richards, one-time wife of a BBC war correspondent, who had been one of the first into Belsen after it was liberated. It was this man's graphic reports that woke a lot of people in Britain and Ireland up to the nature of these camps, changed public opinion, and set the record very straight.

Several of Dublin's 'ladies who lunch' saw *Marrowbone Lane*, and were so touched by the plight of the poor of their city that they set up the Marrowbone Lane Fund. This proposed to use the proceeds of the play and whatever other money they could scrape together to relieve the troubles of these unfortunates.

One of the things they did was to purchase a large house, in which they founded and ran a little home called Fairy

Hill—something between a holiday house and a miniature hospital—for the recuperation of the sick children of these slums. It was decided that we should all be taken there while Bob and his associates searched for homes for Suzi, Terry and Evelyn, and I recovered from my tuberculosis.

Fairy Hill Hospital was located for a number of years in Howth, the large headland that forms the northern end of Dublin Bay. It was at that time a town in itself, though now it is more or less part of the city. The hospital was on the summit of the headland, with lots of fresh sea air and a fantastic view over Dublin Bay, down past Bray Head to the Sugarloaf and the Wicklow mountains. Some say that this area is the Irish answer to the Bay of Naples; others, myself included, say it is better. Bob always maintained that the view, combined with the sea air and a bit of grub, was as good for us as any medication he could have supplied. And I think he was right in that, as in so many other things.

We were taken directly to Fairy Hill from the airport, and finally arrived there fairly late in the evening. It was getting dark. We were all tired and cold, and I was extremely annoyed, because I was not able to see much of what was going on around me. The plaster frame did not help, of course, because it governed all my movements. I must say that I was not very impressed by being in this thing, even if it was for my own good. I was now almost six years old, and becoming a little monster. I still struggled in it, and kept trying to rise—which made me even more uncomfortable and miserable. We were given some bread and warm milk, and bedded down for the night, the lot of us together in the one ward.

Evelyn, Terry and Suzi did not spend much time at Fairy Hill. Evelyn was adopted by a Dublin Jewish family in no time at all. Suzi and Terry followed. They were adopted by the Samuels family, also in Dublin, where they stayed, were schooled, married and had all the rest of a more or less normal life. Evelyn ended up in Australia and prospered in every way. Unlike the rest of us, she traced her family, and was even able to find her father's grave in Chicago. I didn't see her again until about a couple of years ago, when she and her husband came over for a visit. I drove her around Dublin, showed her the sights, and took her around the places where she had spent some of the happier moments of her childhood. We went to visit Han, with whom Evelyn had in fact kept in touch over the years. Sadly, by that time, Han's memory was slipping, and I don't think she had any real idea as to who was visiting. To her, of course, it made no difference, but Evelyn remembered Han as a big part of her childhood, and I think she was disappointed.

After the others were adopted, only Edit and I were left at Fairy Hill. Edit hadn't been affected by the different and assorted afflictions that had been around the camp to the same extent as her brothers. There was nothing the nurses could do for her at this stage, and nothing she could really do to help me in my recovery. Bob decided, therefore, that it would be much better for her if she was to move on, go to our new home, go to boarding school and become a proper little Irish girl.

Initially, she was very anxious about me. It was the first time we had really been separated, and at first she still felt the need to make sure I was all right at all times. Where was I? How was I? Was anybody looking after me? But fortunately, she began to get involved in her own affairs, to settle into school and to make her own friends—whom, I am glad to say, she has to this day. There was a teacher who spoke German at the school she went to, which meant that she was able to blend in without much difficulty.

She came to visit me from time to time, although I am not sure whether that was good for her or not. I think that seeing me may well have been upsetting. The memories must have come flooding back; she must have been struck by our mother's exhortation to mind the boys. Yet at the same time her mind probably got some rest from knowing that I was still around and being taken care of. It was another of life's little paradoxes.

My therapy at Fairy Hill was very much in line with Bob's mentality—plenty of sea air, exercise, and the company of other children. I certainly benefited from the sea air, but I was still kept rigidly immobile by the plaster frame, and was only beginning to learn English. There was no counselling, no therapy or anything like that. Instead of being encouraged to talk about what had happened to us, we were given a clean break. Bob's opinion, and the general medical opinion at the time, was that the best way to recover from a traumatic experience was to ignore it. Forget it, and it will go away. This is very different, of course, from the thinking of today, but I am not so sure that it didn't work. I think that by and large, when I forgot it, it did go away.

At first I found it very difficult to make friends, because I couldn't communicate with the other children. However, I already had three languages—Slovak, Hungarian and German—and I had little trouble picking up a fourth. I was being taught English and I was immersed in it, and there was nobody who really understood my own languages, so English took their place. Soon, English became the usual language even between Edit and myself—except in special circumstances. I remember one time when I was being asked to do something and, not unusually, was refusing. Edit broke in and gave the order in Hungarian. I did it straight away. Granny had spoken Hungarian, and if Granny gave an order, she meant business.

There was a sweet little old lady who used to come up to Fairy Hill to try and teach me English. I remember her trying to teach me my colours using Smarties. We always had a great deal of difficulty with red and green, since the Slovak 'r' sound is very different from the English. Whether or not I was taking the old lady for a ride in order to garner sweets I can't remember, but I certainly ate an awful lot of red and green Smarties before I could say those words. Curiously enough, I never managed to get rid of that rolling 'r', and my accent, which is otherwise completely Irish, still carries a trace of it. Dermot, one of Bob's sons, used to torture me by making me say, 'Round the rugged rock the ragged rascal ran.' I could hardly say it without dribbling all over the place, let alone saying the letter 'r' properly.

———

All this time, the tuberculosis in my spine was incubating quite nicely. At one stage it spread out along a rib, and I had an enormous lump on the left side of my belly, or should I say abdomen. This had to be drained, or should I say aspirated, at regular intervals, which I did not find very pleasant. It involved large thick needles being pushed under my skin. I really was a horrible little boy by now, and in my usual manner would howl as loudly and as long as I thought I could get away with. I felt very sorry for myself and I had decided that at all times I would take any attention that was coming to me, and demand it if it wasn't.

I also developed measles—an ailment which usually costs a child a few days of school, but cost me much more. Few people know, thankfully, that the complications can be quite horrific. I was not in the best of shape to start with, but when I got the measles I went downhill fast. For ten days, I went completely blind.

This is not uncommon, but for me it was the end of the world. My eyes, which I had used to great effect to get what I wanted, were now out of action. Life was a mess. I was still in my plaster frame, which was now propped up on a metal one, again with the necessary aperture for waste. It was a horribly uncomfortable arrangement. I could not move around, I was very sick, in quite a lot of pain, and now my eyes were no use and there were itchy pustules all over my body which I could not scratch.

However, time does have a habit of moving on, and in due course I improved. The measles disappeared; my vision came back, and along with it my smile. It appeared that the tuberculosis, although it had not been cured, had gone into remission. My doctors and nurses felt that I was ready for the next stage. It was time to see what could be done about straightening out my spine.

At this time, as I have said, there was no real cure for TB, although there was much research being done in the area. Four vertebrae in my spine had been affected, and I was becoming a most peculiar shape. There was a bump of quite some size on my back, and it seemed on occasion to slide over to the left. This was not good. The powers that be, or were, felt that in time my chest would be pushed into my diaphragm and this would impinge seriously on my breathing.

There was also the cosmetic aspect of it to worry about. How would I fit in at school? And what about the time when I would discover girls? On that score they need not have worried. As I grew up, most of my female friends were fascinated by this bump, and would gently massage it and ask if it hurt a lot. Of course, it did not hurt at all, but I would wince, pretend to be very brave and say, 'No, not too much.' May God forgive me.

I was moved to what was then the National Orthopaedic Hospital. This was in Clontarf—also a suburb of Dublin, and also on the north side. It is still there, but it has changed, for in the 1960s and 1970s we went through a stage here in Ireland where big was beautiful. A lot of the smaller hospitals were closed down or amalgamated. Nowadays, if you go into one of these new hospitals, you might as well be in an airport.

Back in Fairy Hill I had been king of the castle and, because it was such a small hospital, everyone was used to me and indulged my obnoxiousness. In Clontarf I had to begin all over again. I was at the bottom of the heap. All the other children were older than me, knew each other, and had their own circle of friends. I was the odd one out, and I was not impressed with the fact.

The idea that the powers that be, or were, had for me was to build a kind of corset that I would wear on my back. It would exaggerate the lower curve in my spine, which would compensate for the bump on the upper part of my back. This contraption was a metal frame, covered in hard canvas, with belts, loops and straps. It held my spine rigidly in position. It was also very good for holding the belly in. I could do with it now. It was ugly and heavy, far too hot in the summer, and

One of the huts at Belsen. The conditions shown here are desperately overcrowded, but the British Army cameras did not photograph the worst of them.

© Imperial War Museum

A survivor, discovered by the British when they entered the camp. He is one of the many who were close to death from starvation and disease.

© Imperial War Museum

The thousands of corpses were dragged from the huts and cast into huge burial pits. The numbers were such that the army used bulldozers, not only to dig the trenches that would serve as mass graves, but also to push bodies into them.

Both © Imperial War Museum

A flyer advertising the Belsen Gala Day organised by the liberators.

Edit, a gypsy and myself. This photo was apparently taken in Belsen, after the liberation and the death of our mother.

Luba Tryszynska, the Angel of Belsen, with several Dutch orphans. It was thanks to Luba's ingenious ways of finding extra food that many children, probably including myself, managed to survive.

© *Imperial War Museum*

 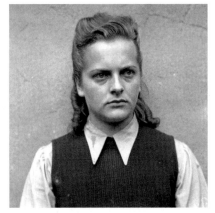

Above left: Commandant Josef Kramer, nicknamed the Beast of Belsen—the man responsible for running the camp in its last dreadful months.

Above right: SS Irma Grese.

Both © Imperial War Museum

The burning of the last of the huts, on 21 May. The former prisoners saw this as a ritual, a cleansing by fire. It was followed by a celebration.

© Imperial War Museum

A group of survivors grieving over a burial pit, now covered with earth. This picture was taken almost exactly a year after the liberation.

© *Imperial War Museum*

Another Belsen survivor, Edit and myself with two nurses during our convalescence in Sweden. Note my famous grin and glossy black hair.

The 'Belsen children photo': a group of weary, airsick children arrive in Ireland. Left to right: Terry, Edit, Suzi, Evelyn and me.

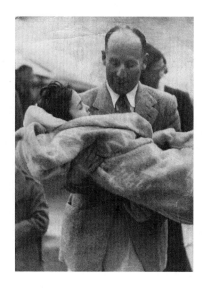

With Bob Collis, my new father, on our arrival at Collinstown Airport, Dublin.

Bob in the Tatra Mountains, on his visit to Slovakia to discover my family and history.

At Fairy Hill Hospital, Howth, near Dublin. According to Bob, the view over Dublin Bay contributed to my convalescence just as much as the treatment.

Robby, Edit, Phyllis, myself and Rusty, the red setter, in the Wicklow mountains near Bo Island.

With Han, Joan and three of our children.

Han and Bob in the 1970s, after their retirement and shortly before Bob's death.

With fellow Belsen survivor Suzi Diamond, 50 years after our liberation. It was about this time that both of us began to speak about our Holocaust experience.

Molly and Adam, two of my grandchildren.

With my family at home in Athy. Left to right: Caroline (aka Woollyhead), Joan, Siobhan, myself, Nichola and Emma.

© Alicia McAuley

caused lots of chafing and itches I could never get at. I hated it. I longed to go running around on the beach, playing ball with the other children. But as it was, I was completely immobile, stretched out on the plaster frame. The corset meant that in theory, I could move around, although for quite a while after it was fitted I was still far too sick to be out of bed.

Whether or not the corset did the job it was meant to do for my spine I cannot say. Now, things are coming a bit unstuck; there are bulging discs and nerves and bumps and lumps which should not be there. But at the time it seemed to be the best thing they could arrange for me. And as it happened, it would have one positive result. I wore it when I finally got to go to school, which was a few years later. Being nearly enough a normal little boy, I got into quite a few normal-little-boy fights. I would go in backwards, and the little fists of my opponent would come into contact with the hard canvas and the belts and buckles. I had my own bullet-proof vest, and unless someone got me in the nose, which bled at the slightest touch, I always won the fight.

It was while I was in Clontarf that my serious love affair with cats began. A stray kitten wandered in one day, a little tabby. He seemed to be afraid of the other children, but for some reason he was not afraid of me, and ended up in my bed, under the covers. He became my pet, and I surreptitiously fed him milk and pieces of my own bread. Telling this, I cannot help but think of the ugly SS guard in Belsen who kept my family alive with her own rations. Perhaps it was the same feeling that motivated her to help us—a feeling of simple kindness, I suppose.

Cat and I were getting on fine, until one day the matron was doing her rounds and heard a purring coming from my bed. At first she was baffled. Who would have a cat in a hospital bed? She must not have known me very well at this stage. She found him, and was about to take him away, but I managed to explain that his purring helped me to go to sleep. Matron, having come up from the country as a young girl, had a sound understanding of human nature, and decided that the cat would be good for me. Like the immigration officials, she managed to look the other way. The cat stayed with me for a while, but then went away, as cats do.

Actually, I owe that matron a lot more than thanks for her tolerance of the cat in my bed. A short time after this, while she was doing her rounds, she noticed that I was holding myself in a rather unusual way, and that my neck seemed to be stiff. Apart from being kind-hearted she was also a damn fine nurse, and she very quickly realised that something was wrong.

She phoned Bob. He suspected the worst, and the tests proved he was right, yet again: tuberculous meningitis. Not a good thing to have at all. From that point I very quickly got sicker and sicker. After a few days, I had grown so weak that it seemed only a matter of time until I would die.

Then fate, or whatever we are going to call this force which runs through my life, stepped in again. Sir Alexander Fleming, the man who had discovered penicillin, just happened to be in Ireland, and Bob, being a big fish in the small pond of Irish medicine, got wind of this. He had heard that Fleming was working on a new drug called streptomycin, which was to be used against tuberculosis. It was still being developed, and its effects were by no means completely understood. No one knew whether it really worked, what the dosage was, or how it should be administered.

But Bob made a few calls, got in touch with Fleming, and managed to get hold of all the streptomycin that Fleming had with him. Then Bob took one hell of a chance—though perhaps not, since I was going to die anyway. He gave me massive doses of streptomycin by injection in the rear. There is no need to say it, but I will anyway: I howled.

Everyone waited anxiously to see what effect the streptomycin would have. If Bob had given me too much, the drug would kill me. If he had given me too little, I would die from the fever. There was only a very slim chance that I would survive. But in a very short space of time, my temperature came down, the stiffness disappeared and I was my usual obnoxious self again. Bob had hit the nail on the head.

They later discovered that one of the side effects of large doses of streptomycin was deafness, and there were a lot of other nasty things that resulted from the wrong dosage. But I survived and suffered no long-term ill effects whatever. Was it fate again? Or just good luck? Or was it just that Bob's medical background allowed him to make an educated guess?

Remember, I did say at the very beginning that I just seemed to have the right people around me at the right time. But might not that have been the work of fate too?

———◆———

After spending a few more months in Clontarf while this corset was being fine-tuned, I went back to Fairy Hill. Fairy Hill was really only meant to cater for children of four to six years old. I was now seven or eight, and so, much older than the rest of the children. For children, up until they are about nine years old, the months of their development, never mind the years, are of enormous consequence. We are, after all, the results of our life experiences, and at those early ages the very smallest and least significant experience has a great bearing on who you are. In even a few months you can become a different person.

By this time, as I have said, I was far too old for Fairy Hill, and cut off from the other children by my age. I was already very obnoxious, but this made me much worse. I don't like having to say that about myself, but it is the truth. I bossed the nurses and the other children around, expecting to be waited on hand and foot. If I did not get my own way, I went into a dark sulk until such time as I thought that people had grovelled enough for me to smile and chuckle again. I wonder if that may be where Gizmo gets his moods from. It is fair to say also that discipline in Fairy Hill was not all that harsh. My Hungarian granny would, as we say in Ireland, soon have put a stop to my gallop.

On the other hand, I suppose, life had not been easy for me. I had lost nearly all my family, had almost been given up for dead several times, was in a strange country and was having to learn a new language. My sister—the last link with what had been my home—had gone away to a place called school. My new father, the consultant paediatrician, would flounce in from time to time in his long white coat, surrounded by people. He would seldom be able to give me his full attention, and so the feelings of abandonment that had visited me in Sweden came back as well. I was a poor little orphan with a big bump on his back and no one to love him. Is it any wonder that I was feeling hard done by, and is it any wonder that my doctors and nurses were indulging me?

So, eventually, I was taken out of Fairy Hill and brought to the National Children's Hospital on Harcourt Street. Bob was a particularly big wheel here, so his fame reflected somewhat on me, and of course I was still a Belsen child. However, by now I was finally learning that the world did not revolve around me. There were other children of my own age group ready to put me in my place if I got too uppity. Bob did say to me once that I was pretty quick on the uptake of things. Just as well.

I was still quite ill. Because I had been in bed so long, my muscles had atrophied. I would just have to learn how to walk again. At the time, this was the cause of some dispute between Bob and myself. He felt that I should stay in bed, as still as possible, so that my vertebrae would have a chance to fuse together. But I had had enough of that. There was no way I was going to stay in bed, and now that I was becoming able to move about, no one could really make me. In the end, as usual, I got my way. Bob never said so, but I am pretty sure he was rather pleased at my efforts. It showed that I still had some fight left in me, which was a very good thing.

———•———

When it was finally decided that I was well enough to leave hospital, I went to live in a large Georgian house on Fitzwilliam Square, south of the river, with Bob, his wife Phyllis, his two sons Dermot and Robby, and Rusty the red setter. Rusty and Edit had already become very firm friends, although for the sake of truth I should say that he would have been friends with anyone who would give him food and attention—much like myself at that time. Suzi tells a sad tale of the time she was brought to see Bob because she had broken out in spots—chicken pox or something like that. Tea was being taken in the drawing room—as always, on a kidney-shaped tray, from a silver teapot and fine china cups and saucers—when Rusty came bustling in. Suzi, who was still very young and very small, was not too sure about this red thing that came sniffing at her. I cannot blame her—in Belsen there had been half-wild dogs all around, which would scavenge the flesh of the dead and the dying. Rusty, of course, was different. It was not her he was sniffing, but rather the slice of cake she was holding aloft in her hand. Being quite a bit bigger, and more experienced where cake was concerned, he wolfed it out of her hand, and by way of a thank you gave her a hard swipe of his wagging tail.

I had been banished from the room, because Suzi had to take off her top. At that age, of course, it would have made no difference to me or to her, but the Victorian manners of the Square demanded it. No one had told me that it was safe to come in, but when I heard Suzi yelp, I thought I should go and investigate. I went into the drawing room and found the dog happily eating the cake and Suzi furious, glowering at him. Of course, I thought this was one of the funniest things ever, and began to chortle riotously. Suzi was not at all impressed. She still throws that in my face on occasions.

In fact, that was the last time I saw Suzi until just a few years ago, when she and I went back to Belsen to film a television documentary. I am pretty sure we were deliberately separated by our respective guardians. Suzi was a reminder of our awful past, and according to Bob, it was best for us not to have any contact at all. And so we didn't.

In the Square, life was good. We wanted for nothing. There was a resident cook and a resident housemaid. We didn't even open the doors of the house for ourselves, but rang the doorbell every day and were let in by a servant. This was the style and custom of living for a man of Bob's class and position, although it may well have been somewhat beyond his means. Bob was never very good at sending out bills, and I believe that more often than not, his bank account was overdrawn.

Meals were taken at the same time every day, and once again I was expected to behave. Nonetheless, there was plenty of fun to be had for a small and adventurous boy, and lots to do. I remember, for example, going to a little boy's birthday party on the other side of the Square. He got a toy boat as a present. So we filled the bath with water so that we could play with the boat and I slopped the water all over the place—much to the annoyance of the boy's parents and the embarrassment of Phyllis.

———

Bob, at this time, was deeply in love with Han, and took every opportunity he could to see her. But he was a man of honour, and he could not lightly throw off his commitment to his wife and his children. He was by nature and nurture forthright and honest, and I am sure that it tortured him to deceive Phyllis. Although his affair with Han continued, Bob remained married to Phyllis throughout the childhood and adolescence of all his children, and Phyllis became, to all intents and purposes, my second mother. Years later, in fact, when Phyllis died, I got a very nice letter from Han saying that she had kept herself deliberately in the background while Phyllis was alive. It was Phyllis, she said, who had reared us, who had brought us up and who had looked after us, and she did not want to divide our loyalties.

Phyllis was in every way a gentlewoman. She came from Cornwall and a similar background to Bob. She was cultured, educated, very kind and very good-natured. She was quiet, liked birds and flowers and animals—but unfortunately for Bob, did not like horses. She did try horse-riding once, but she was really quite small and the horses were large, so it didn't work out at all. Bob, insofar as he was able to look beyond his own nose and how great he was himself, did love her, I imagine. But she was no match for him, either intellectually or physically—and although most probably he did not realise it, he treated her as a doormat.

How she reacted to the idea of taking in two orphaned waifs I do not know, but I imagine she accepted it with her usual unflappable grace. I have a vision in my mind of Bob arriving back from Europe to Fitzwilliam Square, wearing the filthy British Army battledress of which he was very fond, and shouting upstairs to Phyllis, 'I'm home, dear! You'll never guess what I've brought you!' I wonder whether she got a box of Black Magic as well. Probably not.

I grew to respect Phyllis deeply. I am not sure I can say I loved her; she was a lady, an austere British aristocrat. I couldn't climb up into her lap and give her hugs and cuddles like I had been able to do with Luba, but she was good to me. She had a big influence on my life.

Having said that, it was not easy to fit into a new family. Some few years after we arrived in Ireland, we were naturalised, and we changed our surnames from Zinn to Zinn-Collis. But even then, neither Edit nor myself really felt Collis. We always felt Zinn. In terms of the household—the space we took up, the mess we made and the expense necessary to keep us—we would not have made a lot of difference. Anyway, after a short while we were out from under their feet and off to boarding school. But somewhere in the back of my mind I always felt like an imposition on Bob and his family.

I am certain none of them ever saw us as such. The idea never would have dawned on them. They were always impeccably good to us, and still are, and expended great efforts of time and emotion to make us feel part of the clan. Once, I said to Robby, 'Of course, if you were my brother...' He was furious, and rounded on me. 'What the hell do you mean, *if* I was your brother?' I cannot speak for my sister, but for me, the impediments to my really becoming a Collis were of my own making.

But perhaps inevitably, I did feel slightly alienated, especially at first. It would be difficult for any children to settle into somebody else's family, especially at our age. And we had the extra barriers of language, culture and a past full of chaos and destruction. Little by little, though, we became the children of Bob and Phyllis, and the little brother and sister of Dermot and Robby Collis.

Dermot left Ireland for Canada in the mid-1950s, although no one is completely sure why. He was a nice guy, very kind and very clever, but a little vague and quite eccentric. He went to Canada, joined the Air Force, and made his life over there. He was passionate about languages. In fact, he found it difficult to talk about anything else, and he got quite interested in the Inuit at one time. He set about putting together an Inuit telephone directory for the Bell Telephone Company, using a computer from a large Canadian university. Computers at that time were the size of a two-storey semi-detached house, very expensive and very thin on the ground. Needless to say, he didn't have the university's permission—and inevitably, they found out about it in the end. It did not go down very well.

Dermot was never a big factor in my life because as I grew up, he was out of the country. Robby, on the other hand, did everything an older brother should. When I was older, he taught me how to drink, he taught me about the birds and the bees, and with the greatest patience in the world he taught me to drive. I was not the quickest learner in that regard. Once, I turned into Fitzwilliam Square from Leeson Street at about 50 miles an hour, clipping a lamp post and almost running over a few pedestrians. Robby did not so much as flinch, and when we stopped, he said only, 'Next time maybe a little bit slower.' And that was it.

In many ways Robby was a father to me as well. Bob's was a public life. He had a huge heart, but it manifested itself best in the expansive arena of communities, cities and even countries. His private life, it could be said, suffered as a result. With his own sons, as with Edit and me, he was always somewhat vague, somewhat distant—always more of a father figure than a father. I do not wish to disparage him: he was always kind, never cruel and never neglectful, and we always had the unspoken and unexplained bond that had been present since Belsen.

However, I cannot say that we were close in the conventional sense, and I never really had any meaningful conversations with him. One day we were driving along St Stephen's Green, and there was a man walking alongside the car in a most peculiar fashion. He was half limping, half waddling along. Bob saw that I was watching him, looked at me and said matter-of-factly, 'He's got syphilis. That is what happens if you go with too many women.' And that was the extent of the sex education Bob gave me. Robby had a much better take on it—but I will come to that in due course.

I can remember Bob sitting on his bed one Monday morning in the Square. He was fully dressed except for one shoe and sock. The shoe was in his hand, and he was proclaiming at the top of his voice, 'I am not going anywhere until someone finds my sock!' And there he sat, stubbornly. He was sitting on his sock. We all knew it, but none of us was brave enough to tell him, so we all rushed around pretending to search for it.

What a contradiction he was. Tender and gentle, picking me up and discovering a bump on my back, then an austere and dignified Victorian father, and then this ogre who couldn't find his sock. He was a man of many parts. But no matter what situation he was in, he was always the boss—always at the top of the food chain. He never pulled rank—there was no need. He just was.

Bob never talked about Belsen to me or to Edit. It just wasn't mentioned. It never happened. But I pass no judgement on him for that. As he saw it—and there is logic in the idea—it would have been just too disruptive to us. How can you talk to an eight, ten, 14, 16-year-old boy about the concentration camps with their gassings, hangings, shootings and beatings? How could you expect such a boy to keep on going to school, to keep on doing what he is doing? In some ways it is unfortunate. Perhaps there are conversations that we should have had but never did. But he meant well, and what is done cannot be changed now.

As for myself, I never tried not to think about Belsen. I never consciously blocked it out of my mind. But nevertheless, it went. From then until I was in my mid-50s, it seldom crossed my mind. Even now, after I have thought about it often and deeply, and spoken about it again and again, I still find it difficult to grab hold of the memory. I know all these things happened. I remember them. But I do have trouble connecting this film reel in my mind with my present-day reality. That orphaned urchin, playing around the rotting bodies—was it really me? Perhaps that has something to do with having ignored the whole thing for so long. I do not know what a psychologist would say about that, but I think it was good for me to forget, even if temporarily. I could try to make up for the portion of my childhood I had lost. I could get on with my life.

———

By 1949, I was almost nine years old, and I still had not been to school. I had had a few tutors since I had come to Ireland, with varying degrees of success. There was the lady with the Smarties, as well as some others who used more conventional methods of teaching, such as making me pay attention and do assignments. These methods I did not agree with, so my progress was not great. Something that did work, though, was bribery. My reading skills at that time were very poor, but not for nothing was Bob a paediatrician. He had the measure of me, and hit on the idea of bribing me with the promise of a clockwork Hornby train engine. If I was able to read a certain piece of writing by a certain date, the engine would be mine. He bought the tracks and carriages, and kept them in the house as a tantalising encouragement.

There was never such a bright and diligent student as I was until I had this treasure in my hand. The engine was something else. It even had a reverse gear. I took very well to reading after that. I soon discovered that if you read, you can be anyone and do anything, anywhere. And once I learned, I never stopped, and never needed to be bribed again.

Despite my progress, school was now becoming a serious issue. Edit had gone to the Quaker boarding school in Waterford, and it was time for me to join her. But it was already after Christmas by the time I left hospital, and after a few months in Fitzwilliam Square it was decided that there was no point sending me away that school year. For the summer term I was sent to a little prep school on Leeson Street, just around the corner from our house in the Square.

That school, which I believe was and still is called Dr Stevens, was run very much along the lines of a British prep school. The headmaster, as far as I can remember, was a real Mr Chips type—old, kind and very wise. The rest of the staff, I think, were students. There was order, routine, a timetable and a uniform. The uniform consisted of a very smart black blazer, grey knee socks and shirt, a smart tie, a bright red cap—and, of course, grey short pants. I soon found that it was possible to pee out the leg of these short pants without having to undo any buttons, which would have taken up precious time. This, of course, was in the days before zip flies. Nine times out of ten, despite my metal corset, I managed to bring this off without accidents. It must be terrible for the boys of today, with their long-legged trousers.

There was one day, a Monday, when I had been in a hurry to get ready and had got dressed without paying much attention to my socks. I arrived to school wearing a pair of Edit's, which were bottle green. This was a cause of much merriment to my classmates, and never have I been in the wrong get-up since, whatever the occasion. Funny the things that stay with you and shape you. For me, it was the fire hose in Belsen, the gallows, and a pair of bottle-green socks. Events of the most enormous historical importance, and events of the smallest significance. The horrific and the utterly banal, side by side.

I didn't take very well to games either. It was the summer term, and the sport of choice was cricket. In cricket, of course, unless you are batting or bowling, nothing much ever happens on the field of play. One day, I was silly-mid-on or square leg or maybe even third man. Whatever position I was supposed to be, I was in a little world of my own—and it was not on the cricket field. Out of the blue a cricket ball, which like all cricket balls was really rather hard, hurtled towards me and slammed into the side of my head. I refused point blank ever to go near that field again, and I haven't ventured near one since.

I was in that school for only one term, and then it moved out to what then would have been suburbia. Property prices in Leeson Street were going, as it were, through the roof, and the pool of potential students would have been drying up. All the big houses in the area, which had been occupied by high-powered lawyers and doctors like Bob and from which most of the students would have come, were becoming offices. Many of the consultants were given rooms for their private practices in these new hospitals which looked like airports, and the families moved out into the allegedly healthier suburbs. The school moved out with them, and I moved on to Waterford.

———•———

Newtown. What a place! What a school! I said at the beginning that after my rocky start in this world, I have been very lucky in the people who have come my way and the places I have ended up in; Sweden, Fairy Hill, the Square, and now the place that has had perhaps more influence on me than any other.

Newtown is a co-educational boarding and day school in the city of Waterford, on the south-east coast of Ireland. It has been on the go for over 200 years, run by the Religious Society of Friends, or the Quakers.

I was there for all of my schooling, apart from my brief spell in the school of the short pants, the bottle-green socks and the cricket ball, and I believe that I received there the most rounded education it was possible to receive at that time. At Newtown, education was not a question of exposing you to books and hoping that learning would happen. The Quaker teachers took the view that every child was good at something. It might be mowing playing fields or rugby or chess or classical languages, but there was always something. It was up to them, as educators, to find out what that something was, and to foster the spark of talent within the child. And for the most part they succeeded—there is a long line of former Newtown pupils who went on to diverse and momentous achievements.

During my time there, the school had only about 100 boarders and about half that number of day pupils. Newtown was way ahead of the rest of Ireland as regards the equality of the sexes, and the gender mix was kept half and half, by design. It was a very close community in terms of background and class. One night, by complex calculation, we were able to work out how every single person in the school was related to everybody else, including Edit and myself, taking marriage and adoption into account. Quite literally, Newtown was a family.

It was rigorously ordered and fair in every way, and the Quaker influence was everywhere to be seen. The Quakers believe in tolerance, justice, and above all, honour. I remember one horrendous instance one morning at roll call. Somebody had had a pair of shoelaces stolen—and there was absolute murder about it. 'This is really letting the side down,' they said. 'One mustn't do these sorts of things.' Now, in these cynical days, reproofs like these seem so naïve, but at the time we all took it extremely seriously.

One night, I and a few others went to visit the girls' dormitories to raid the kitchens. We were caught, and the staff quite rightly gave us a long and harsh dressing down. They all had a go at us—every one, except my form master. Of all the teachers I was most terrified of what he would have to say, but all he did was look at me over his half-moon spectacles, shake his head and say, 'Foolish, foolish boy.' And that—his disappointment—affected me more than all of the other teachers' remarks put together.

By and large, we were disciplined by instruction rather than punishment, and what punishment there was at Newtown was comparatively light. It generally took the form of order and conduct marks. Four order marks equalled half an hour's detention on a Saturday afternoon; five meant 45 minutes; six was the equivalent of a conduct mark—one hour. These marks were put opposite our names on a list on the common notice-board.

There was no corporal punishment, although there was a maths teacher with the unfortunate name of Boggs, who was not above using the sole of his slipper to put manners on us. He used to sleep in the school and would regularly catch us talking after lights out. On one occasion during my first term at Newtown he caught five of us, and duly called us to his office. The slipper was applied—ten or twelve whacks each. I was still used to being mollycoddled in Fairy Hill and the Square, and I was shocked that I was actually about to be punished for something. I was the last one in line, and when

Boggs got to me he paused. I don't know whether he was getting tired at this stage or whether he took pity on me, but I only got two. At the back of it all, he was a compassionate man, and over the years we developed a sort of grudging respect for each other.

When it came to eating, the dinner tables seated eight, and each had to have four boys and four girls. The two pupils at either side of the end would have to clear the plates for the wash-up ladies, and everyone moved one place around the table each day. If it was your turn at the top of the table, you got to use the milk first for your porridge, and you got the creamy liquid at the top—except for one table, which was presided over by Boggs. He would stir the milk first, use it, then pass it around. We also had to move one table each week, in order to facilitate a quick exit when the meals were over.

Considering the profession I took up, it would be kinder not to pass comment on the actual meals. They were adequate, if not very large—or so it seemed, but as my four daughters have taught me, young people tend to be hungry most of the time anyway. Every Sunday, though, we would have a sticky bun. Sunday was a good day to be at the top of the table, for as well as the top of the milk you also got first pick of the buns. Sometimes, if you weren't so lucky, it would be possible to trade one for another.

I was nine years old when I started at Newtown, and I had only had one term's worth of proper education. Nonetheless, I must have been fairly smart because I caught up quickly.

Academically, I didn't excel exactly, but I was able to hold my own. I was never first, but it wasn't very long until I was hovering around the second, third and fourth places in the class. I managed to get a very good grasp of English very quickly, and that made the rest pretty easy.

I enjoyed Latin. I enjoyed all the classical subjects, in fact, and I was good at them. My Latin teacher was called Bam (he was so named because he used to make us recite verbs again and again—*amo, amas, amat, amamus*, and somewhere in there, there is an *abamus*). When the time came for the Intermediate Certificate exam, Bam told me, 'Go in for it, you might get something.' From him this was the height of praise, and I was delighted. He taught senior English as well, which I enjoyed immensely. I tried music, but I was more interested in playing it the way I thought it should sound rather than the way it was written. Maths I couldn't do at all, but then I had had very little by way of previous instruction in that area. Nevertheless, I was spurred into trying very hard by Boggs and his ubiquitous slipper.

They were happy days I spent at Newtown. It was overwhelming, but this time in a good way. I was no longer a displaced person. I belonged. These rituals, habits, customs that we had made Newtown a community, and one that Edit and I were part of this time. I think this was an immense help for us. Through the routines of Newtown, we were able to meld into an equitable society—a healthy one, and a happy one. We looked different from the other children, we sounded different, and everyone there would have been aware of our background. Yet we were treated exactly the same. We were not special, we were not set apart, but we were important, indispensable and valued. That was the wonderful thing about the school.

I was so valued, in fact, that at one stage I was made the official bell ringer. The bell was outside, and I had to pull a chain a particular number of times, depending on the time of day. It was a great honour to be appointed. The bell ringer had a grave responsibility and was therefore someone to be looked up to. The whole school depended on me to keep time, after all. But more importantly, I got out of class a few minutes early so that I could set my watch to school time. The main part of the school was an old Georgian house, and there was a big grandfather clock in the hall. I don't know if it ever told the right time, but this was the clock by which school time was determined. I would be there every morning at half past seven setting my watch, and every morning, Boggs would be there doing the same. I would run past him like the clappers, off to ring the bell, and we would nod a resentful acknowledgement at each other.

I had another job too. I became the chief playing-field cutter. The headmaster of the time, like Bob, was a great believer in the power of fresh air to keep you healthy, in mind and as well as in body. So in all weathers and circumstances, everybody had to go outside every afternoon for about an hour and a half. Four days a week this time would be taken up by playing games. Another two days there would usually be a match of some sort. And on Sunday, if your parents were not down to feed you, you could have a picnic and go off on bicycles.

I was not allowed to play rugby because of my back, though I am sure I would have loved it. Imagine a scrum with that harness on. Strangely, though, they did let me play a rather vicious game on roller skates, where you would get down on your hunkers and have someone push you into another boy in the same position. The one who did not fall was the winner. I was quite good at this. Being smaller, my centre of gravity was low, and my pusher was very good. Hockey I liked, though I played with more enthusiasm than skill, and after Leeson Street I refused even to entertain the idea of taking part in a cricket game. Much of the time, therefore, I could not or would not play the games, and quite often I found myself at a loose end during this time outside.

The senior master, who had charge of all things sporting, was a Mr Foster. His initials were F.E.F., and so, of course, he was universally called Fef. For your first term at school he would appear very fierce, cross and wicked, and you would avoid him as best you could. For a while with new arrivals he would try to be all of these things, but he could never keep a straight face while doing so. By term two you would have the measure of him.

Nonetheless, Fef was a fine teacher in that he knew his pupils. He was a nice guy and, dare I say it, a role model for us. And when it came to games, he was having none of my nonsense. I was not about to spend an hour and a half each day sitting around. I was to have my fresh air, and he had an idea as to how I could be put to good use.

One day, he took me and stood me in front of the motor mower, the second best one to begin with. He showed me how to start and stop it, and then just told me to get on with it. There were expanses of rugby pitch, lawns and grass verges all the way around the school, and I tore over them with my mower like a Formula One driver around a racing track. I was chief bell ringer and in charge of a motor mower. And I got out of running around after stupid little balls and being walloped with sticks and bats. What more could you want at that age? To make it even better, at the end of each term, Fef would slip me a few half crowns—a lot of money for a small boy in those days.

The headmaster for most of my time at Newtown was a man by the name of Mr Glynn. He was another of the beneficent gentlemen with whom I was lucky enough to come into contact. He had driven Red Cross ambulances and carried stretchers during the First World War, as had a lot of Quakers who refused to sign up in the armed forces. We gleaned this information for ourselves: it would never, ever cross Mr Glynn's mind to brag about his exploits. He was fluent in Irish and French, although he did not spend a lot of time in the classrooms. His instruction was much more subtle and longer lasting than that of most teachers. I knew him 40-something years ago, and I can still remember many of the things he taught me—his very words, in fact. I would guess that the same goes for most of my schoolmates.

Mind you, Mr Glynn did have a major fault in our eyes. He insisted that we all chew each morsel of food 32 times—16 times on one side of your mouth, and 16 times on the other. While you were still in short pants and newly arrived, this was the source of endless complaint. It was an especial nuisance if you were in a hurry to get out on a fine day, because you would be there for a while.

A few years ago I was doing a course on 'how to be nice to people', or 'finding your inner self', or some such thing. I am not sure just what it was; I was conned into going. Anyway, one of the things they made me do was to name a person who had had a significant influence on my life. Mr Glynn was the man I chose. He led by example and in spite of yourself you tended to follow him, without being aware until much later what was going on. When he retired he married his secretary, to the joy of past and current pupils. He died a few years ago after a very long, fruitful and happy life. I am sure that whichever god happens to be up there will be good to him.

As you must realise by now, that school and I got on very well together. While I was never all that keen on the book-learning part of my education, Newtown taught me patience and tolerance for others—qualities that are now so necessary to be content in this world—and as far as that was concerned I was an able and enthusiastic student. Also, I am quite sure that the exposure I was given there to the Quaker way of life—humanitarian, enlightened, broad-minded and just—has helped me to understand and come to terms with what has been done to me. It is thanks to this ethos that I have no bitterness about my experience in Belsen. I do not feel resentful or vengeful towards the Nazis, the Germans or anyone else, despite the fact that most people expect me to. What happened to me happened to lots of other people. In fact, it is still happening. I just happened to be in the vicinity of the fan when the shit hit it, and I got splattered. But that does not give me the urge to go and bomb all the German cities again. Thanks to the influence of Newtown school, I have accepted what happened to me and moved on with my life. That is no small achievement.

———

For the duration of each summer and at every opportunity during the year, the family went to Bo. Bo Island, to be correct.

At the end of the war, Bob, having come back to Ireland, was looking for a new house. He decided that he wanted to be a gentleman farmer. With a bit of luck he could run this place at a very slight loss, so that the tax man would not get everything. It would double up as a holiday home for his family and a place to keep the odd horse or four.

He and Robby were out riding one day in the Wicklow mountains, I suppose on horses from a livery stable, when they came across a small cottage, surrounded by trees climbing up out of a bog. I think that may be where the 'Island' part came from. Where 'Bo' came into the naming I have no idea, although *bó* is the Irish for cow. He loved the house, and bought it for a song.

At the time, it was a rather typical Irish country farmhouse. Bob told the story that it had been built for the retirement of an Irish racehorse, which had ended up in India belonging to someone of fierce importance. The story goes that this horse won every race he ever took part in, made a lot of money for this fiercely important man, and at the end of his days retired to Ireland with his groom. The groom slept at one end of the house, the horse at the other, and they both lived happily ever after. I would not like to comment on just how true that is, but I heard the tale many times up there when Bob had some people out to visit and a few whiskies in his belly. Mind you, Bo was such a wonderful, magical place, it just might have been true.

When Bob first bought Bo, he had the stables and farm sheds incorporated into the main house. That gave two extra bedrooms and a sitting room, where Bob would write, and in the early days he would read to us all. I used to sit on a bit of the fender at the side of a huge open fireplace, from which billows of turf smoke would come down if the wind was blowing from the wrong direction, which was most of the time. If you put your head into the fireplace (when the fire was out) you could see the sky. I would put up with sitting there, being gently cured by the smoke, because that was really the only way to keep warm. The Wicklow mountains, even in summer, are not the warmest of places.

It was damp, always. We used to keep what we called our Bo clothes out there, and steam would always rise up off them when we put them on. We had no electricity; there were oil lamps for the big ones, and candles for the little ones. We did have a bathroom and running water, most of the time. The water came from a spring on the hill above the house, and the supply system was just a plastic pipe held by rocks under the water. If we had a dry summer, then we had no water. Simple as that. Luckily enough, dry summers were few and far between.

The frogs were quite fond of this spring. They would spawn there, so there would be lots of them. Inevitably, every now and then a small frog or a large tadpole would find its way into the pipe and block it. This used to be a real nuisance. We would have to dig up the pipe and test it with a small nail and a box of matches. The nail was used to make holes at intervals along the pipe. Sooner or later we would find a point where water would begin to squirt out. The offending amphibian would be between this point and the last dry hole.

The amphibian having been removed, we would go back along the pipe, sticking matches in the holes we had made. Then the whole lot would be covered up again until the next time. Dermot, I think, eventually had the bright idea of putting a filter on the spring end of the pipe. Problem solved—until the pipe froze.

We also had a telephone—the only one at that time within a radius of several miles. It was one of those wind-up-the-handle contraptions. Bob, being a doctor, had to have one, and the locals used to come up to use it. We would come back and find a pile of coins by the phone.

There was a proper turf shed, which had to be filled each summer. The little one—me—would have to spend hours in the hot dusty shed, while the others would throw the turf in at me to stack. This turf would be cut from the bog. It was not very good—all the good stuff was long gone by the time we got there. That racehorse must have been fine and warm.

There was also what we called a dairy. We would skim the milk to collect the cream, and after a few days Phyllis would sit down at the churn with a book, and she would churn away. She sat there reading for hours, while this cream was turned into butter, with hair, straw, little flies, bits of fluff and other morsels which were rather hard to identify. This practice eventually stopped. It could be that the books she had were not that good, or that we would often go to the dairy and find the cats having a go at the cream. Bob, despite all his training and skills, was firmly of the opinion that a little bit of clean dirt did no harm at all. I think he was quite right.

The first of my many summers at Bo was after my term at the prep school on Leeson Street. Up until then I had been the most important person in my life, and in the lives of everyone else, or so I thought. Even at the prep school I had been someone of note. After all, the war had not been over all that long, I was foreign, I had a thing on my back which was very hard if you happened to hit it during a squabble—and, it seemed, I had a penchant for bottle-green socks.

Up at Bo life was very different. I had been there before for a weekend, but at that time I was still not very well, and had managed to have everyone running around after me as usual. Now I was quite a bit better. This time, when we arrived, Bob's eldest son Dermot came to help unload the baggage from the car, and managed to spill my new Meccano set in a cascade all over the driveway. Being the little brat I was, I said some rather nasty things to him. I am glad to say I can not remember what they were, but he was not one bit impressed. He spat something back at me, and left me to pick the bits up myself. Not too easy when you can't really walk, never mind bend down.

Now, I am again at the stage where, were I to bend down, getting up again might present some problems, so I can appreciate how outraged I must have been. Upon mature reflection, this was the bit of reality I needed at the time. Needless to say, I did not hold that view then. But as Bob has said, I was quick on the uptake, and I did not hold a grudge any more than Dermot did.

Again, I decided that bed was not the place to be. Everyone else was constantly very busy doing farm work, and did not seem to have much time for my entertainment. The only way to command their attention was to join them. I would scramble out of bed and, by holding on to various bits of furniture, manage to make it to the door. For a long time, getting to the door was an achievement on its own. At this stage my muscles had still not recovered from their long period of inertia; it was quite painful and extremely frustrating to teach my body to move again. But gradually I succeeded, and after a while I was able to join in some of the farmyard fun.

It was my job, as the youngest, to light the fires in the morning and bring Bob and Phyllis their early-morning tea. Then it was breakfast time, but after that I could disappear for the whole day.

A spot I found for myself in time was a little stream at the bottom of the furry field, so called on account of its profusion of gorse bushes. This stream became a harbour, a waterfall, the Shannon, the Amazon, the Nile or all five oceans. Wherever and however Man found water, I had it in this field. For hours on end it would just be me, the field, the water and a pair of wellies that were too big—for as is usual with the youngest, I got the hand-me-downs. With some more of this mature reflection, I think it was just as well that they were too big. Wellies that are the right size are almost impossible to put on when they are damp, and these were damp all the time.

I would dam the stream, and send it this way, then that. I would sail leaves down it—boats which were going to far off lands. I would dig big ponds, and they became lakes with monsters at the bottom. My freedom was limited only by my imagination. I would only go up to the house when I was hungry, or else when Phyllis, who had one hell of a loud voice for a refined lady, used it to call us in.

Phyllis was one of the most inventive cooks I have known, and I worked as a chef for 40 years. She could, and did, make a meal out of anything, almost always using only what we grew at Bo. We had made a vegetable garden out of one corner of the top field, and there we grew most of the vegetables and fruit we could eat. We had hens, and therefore eggs, though there was always a test of skill to see if we could find out where the hens were laying before Rusty, the red setter, who was partial to an egg or three, got there before we did.

Rusty and Edit were now inseparable, as she and the cat had been in Slovakia. Quite often he would sleep on the end of her bed, and quite often this would be the subject of impassioned dispute—because he made an excellent hot-water bottle. Mind you, if I lost the bid to get him for the night, I soon found consolation in one fact: poor Rusty suffered a good deal from wind.

We also had a good many cats at Bo, most of which were named after sea areas—the ones they use for the shipping forecast. At one time we had at least a dozen. A few of them had a habit of sitting not on, but in the hearth, and by consequence they used to get singed quite bald. Now and then Bob would try and give them a shot of some antibiotic. This would be a real family bonding opportunity. The cat had to be wrapped in a towel and held still while Bob tried to insert a needle into the loose skin at the back of its neck. A lot of advice would be offered as to who was going to hold which end of the cat, and how and when. Then, without fail, the cat would get away, Bob would inject himself with the antibiotic, and those holding the cat would get a pawful of claws for their troubles. Family life can be difficult.

Bob loved Bo, and enjoyed every minute of the time we spent there. There is one occasion among many which comes to mind that will demonstrate this very clearly. It was during a school holiday at Easter, which was particularly early that year. For some reason only Bob, Edit and myself were there. Bob usually kept religion for special occasions and, Easter being one of them, we went along to the local church. We sat through the service, Bob growling all the hymns in every key other than the one the rest of us were using. He was completely tone deaf. But he did have a great enthusiasm when he went to church. If places in heaven are given out on the basis of effort, he should have no trouble getting there. Accordingly, he paid very close attention to the sermon. I don't know what verse of the Bible the rector had chosen to use as his starting point, but it concerned a parent's duty to his or her children, and no doubt vice versa. Bob took it very much to heart.

On Easter Monday morning, he dragged Edit and me out of bed before dawn to go for a picnic on the top of a nearby mountain—on horseback. It was pitch dark, we had no flask, and we would have to light a fire with the clouds still sitting on top of the mountain. This we finally managed to do, after many damp boxes of matches. Shivering and miserable, we drank our cold tea with twigs, bits of bushes, and drowned flying things in it. We ate our half-cooked sausages and rashers, but gave up on the eggs because there was too much dirt in the pan. Bob beamed and chattered the whole time.

We went to find the horses to go home, and they had disappeared. This always happened wherever we went, but on top of a mountain in the half-light and mist it was just too much. We found them in the end, or rather they found us, and we limped home and back to bed. Bob felt great for weeks—convinced beyond a shadow of a doubt that he was a wonderful father.

———•———

One of these summers, when I was in my early teens, Robby decided I should learn a little more about farmyard life, and how it could also apply to humans. We had an old cow, who was so ugly that she never did get a name. She had horns, one of which went up and the other down, and she was cross-eyed. Her tail was a rather sad appendage, with a little ball of hair on the end of it.

This particular year, she required the services of a bull, and as it happened there was a rather handsome example of such a creature along the way. So Robby tied a rope around the one-up-one-down horns of this sad-looking cow and set off to meet this fine-looking bull. It was the start of the holiday. Flies were buzzing around with great interest in the cow and in us, the birds were singing and the grass was green. The three of us ambled along the road until we came to the field where the bull and his owner were waiting. The bull seemed to think that our cow was of wondrous beauty, for he gave a bellow of joy upon seeing her and came to inspect her more closely.

Robby and the farmer stayed in a corner of the field and talked nervously about the weather, the price of livestock, the last night's *céilí*—anything except the imminent coupling. I found a gorse bush and began to count the flowers on it, and the cow and the bull did what they were supposed to do.

When the union was complete, Robby had another idea. Now that I knew about cows and bulls, and by extension about girls and boys, I should also find out about drinking. We hitched the cow up again and continued on the road to Roundwood, our nearest village. Actually, it claims to be the highest in Ireland, with the highest pub. Upon arriving there we tied the cow to a railing in front of a window of the highest pub in Ireland and went in. I was well under age, but in those days that was not really a problem. Several bottles of stout later, we collected our cow and headed for home. On leaving the pub Robby said to me, 'Now you know all about life.' In fact I knew a fair bit before that, but this was official.

Robby is now a psychiatrist in Hawaii. If he is the same with his patients as he was with me, I think he must be a very good one.

———•———

In the early days at Bo, we had a farm worker, Leo. He was as strong as they come and, as is quite often the case, as gentle as could be. He became Edit's good friend and mentor. He taught her to waltz in what we called the middle shed, where we kept the oats for the horses. When Leo left us, he went to England and became a mental nurse. He came to visit a few times, with a most elegant wife in tow.

Leo taught Edit how to ride horses, with a few disasters along the way. Robby took over that chore after a while, and also began to teach me. The first lesson was a simple one. He waited until Mike, a workhorse, had finished for the day and was being unharnessed. Then he simply threw me up on Mike's back and waited to see what would happen—although I think he probably knew. Mike, who had delusions of grandeur despite his hairy legs, took off like a Derby winner and kept going till he got to his stable. Luckily, his back was rather like a camel's hump, inverted. Or perhaps I should say it was like mine, inverted. At any rate it was impossible to fall off and I managed to reach the stable in one piece. There is no blame attached to old Mike for this. It was the end of his working day, and the oats were waiting.

I was terrified, but exhilarated. In fact, it was rather like that every time I went to ride from then on. I was not very good, and there were numerous close encounters between my backside and the furry field, but I always found it such fun that I would get up immediately and go again.

When I was a little older we had another horse, who went by the name of Henry. Henry also had notions. He was sure that he was a thoroughbred racehorse and would act accordingly. He would dance sideways, shake his mane, rear up a bit, and generally let you know that he was of some standing in the horse world. But he was a joy to ride, and being the little scoundrel that I was, I learned to use his misbehaviour to my advantage.

By the time we got Henry I had discovered girls. For the most part, of course, they liked the horses, and I would often invite my current lady friend out for a visit. She would be mounted on another horse, called The Tinker, who had no notions of any kind, and was happy just to be a horse. I would make a great show of trying to get up on Henry, who would play his part to perfection. He would dance and trot around in a circle while I would hop after him on one foot, the other one in the stirrup. When I did get into the saddle, he would do a couple of back-leg kicks and a rear or two. My lady friend would be most impressed. All this and a bump on the back as well. How could I not be impressive?

As I got older, though not much bigger, I would do my share of the work around the place. I helped set the potatoes, and became a champion at thinning turnips. Being low to the ground I could scoot along on my knees. I got to be on first-name terms with some of the bugs and crawlies that live down at that level. In the summer, the whole family and all the neighbours worked together saving the hay for the horses, moving from one farm to the next. It was part of the summer ritual, and always ended with us all going in to the tea, sandwiches and sweet apple cake. Of course, it was very funny to move the ladder and leave me on top of the haystack until there were only cheese sandwiches left.

Despite the fact that we were blow-ins from Dublin and that Edit and myself were blow-ins from much further afield altogether, we were really part of the community at Bo, and Bob and Phyllis often organised food and entertainment for the local people. In the early days, Bob would have an elaborate children's Christmas party every year. He would put the squeeze on friends and acquaintances, of whom there were many, for goodies for this event. The locals would come parading up the avenue, which was about half a mile long, with a goose under their arm for the Doctor. As we had a lot of trees around us, we would top one for a Christmas tree, which we would then decorate with tiny candles. Highly dangerous, when I think back on things. It is one of the new wonders of the world that we never set the house on fire, between the cats in the ashes and the candles on the trees.

Father Christmas would also come to these parties. One year Bob bullied his then-current houseman from Harcourt Street Hospital to take on this role. Old Mike, an old set of deer antlers tied to his head, was to play the part of Rudolph. This aspiring medic had never been on a horse before. In fact, I maintain that he had never even seen one. He had found it necessary to take a very large dose of Dutch courage, either out of a bottle or an ether mask.

Both Mike and medic were led halfway down the avenue. The idea, a good one at the time, was that I would sound a car horn and turn on the headlights, and Rudolph and Father Christmas would come galloping along. Sadly, Mike was anything but gracious about this travesty of his God-given form, and did not enter into the spirit of things. Startled by the horn, he managed to shed both the antlers and the medic, and galloped straight past the crowd and into his stable. To the cheers of all the children, Santa limped back, holding his sack with one hand and his behind with the other. I think the medic's peers were not kind to him when he went back to work, for word of his exploits was the talk of all the hospitals in Dublin.

During the first few of these parties at Bo, I was not very happy, and neither was Edit. Being in a confined space with all these children about us stirred up all sorts of things in our minds. The pushing, the shoving, the milling around had shades of the cattle trucks, and of the barrack huts in Belsen. Speaking for myself, I could not drive that uneasiness from my mind, and only wanted to get away. But this was always momentary. For most of the time at Bo I was surrounded by space, freedom and family. I loved it.

What a place for two battered kids to regain a bit of peace and normality. There were some fierce squabbles of course, but is that not what family is all about? We tested ourselves, asserted ourselves, tested the others, and eventually found our place. And we thrived in it. Freedom. We were able to get up in the morning and spend the day almost exactly as we pleased. We were able to be ourselves, and not have to worry about dead bodies, hunger, beatings or bashings. We were able to go to bed at night, exhausted from the fun of the day, and knowing that tomorrow would be the same. I think that, in fact, is the key. Knowing. Certainty.

At Bo, Edit and I were able to put some of our insecurities to one side. They were not being got rid of—I don't think that will ever happen for either of us—but between what we had come from and where we were, there was such a major difference that it is very hard to comprehend just how magical it was to us. We were just being children, and it was wonderful. Bo was a fantastic place, and we were both very lucky to have had a chance to experience it.

The house was eventually burnt down, though not while we were the owners. I have seen it since it was rebuilt; sadly, it is not the same at all. There are doors and windows that actually open, curtains that match and a brand new pump house. It is civilised. Mind you, Uto, Han's nephew, has a fantastic house on the land, with dogs and hens and birds, muddy boots in the hall and ponds to play or swim in. Not quite Bo—still a bit too clean and orderly—but pretty near.

———•———

So the years passed and I grew up, with the twin benefits of the freedom of Bo and the discipline of Newtown. There was only one major interruption to my contentment.

It was Easter 1953, and I was almost 13 years old. I had by now spent a few years at Newtown and was as usual dividing the holiday between Bo and the Square. The day before we were due back to school, as was the custom, Phyllis, Edit and myself went into Dublin to see the latest movie. This year it happened to be *Quo Vadis*. After the film, we began to walk the short distance back to the Square. As we were crossing O'Connell Bridge, I coughed up a pint of blood into the Liffey—with no warning to myself or anybody else. I tried to catch the blood in my brand new green handkerchief— which, of course, went straight into the river and floated off out of sight. I think I was more dismayed at the loss of the handkerchief than at whatever was wrong with me this time. Phyllis and Edit carted me back to the Square, and I was summarily shoved off to bed to await the arrival of the big man.

Bob arrived, quite flustered. Ever since I had been in the various hospitals before starting school, everyone—even Bob—had believed that my TB had pretty much cleared up. But that was the most likely cause of what was happening to me. Frantically, x-rays and blood tests were taken. I was poked with needles and made to swallow many and varied revolting potions. What for I do not know, but they even tried to put a rubber tube down into my stomach while I was wide awake. This was too much. I was having none of that, thank you very much. I did not quite resort to my Fairy Hill tactics of pique and tantrums, but pique and tantrums were not far away. In the end there was only one way they were going to be able to get these tubes into me. They took me into Harcourt Street Hospital and knocked me out.

Sure enough, the tuberculosis was back. It had not disappeared, but had been simmering away all this time in my spine. Nobody had suspected that it was still there, let alone that it had been spreading over the years, but that was the truth of it. Now, TB was rampant in my chest and my life was once again in grave danger.

Immediately, I was put on all the new drugs that had come into use after the discovery of streptomycin by my old pal Sir Alexander Fleming. Some of them were injected, but others I had to take by mouth, including a substance called PAS. I had to take two tablespoonfuls every hour and a half. It was absolutely foul, and left an aftertaste that no amount of Easter egg could remove—and believe me, I tried. I can still taste it. They gave me another drug called INAH, and they also gave me streptomycin—more needles in the backside. This time, though, they knew the dosage and were not going to kill me or make me deaf.

However, none of these drugs worked, and as I became sicker I took to bed in the Square. The weekends at Bo went on for the family, and I was left at the mercy of the resident help—and Phyllis's mother, who was still alive and living on the top floors of the house. She was ancient, and felt that eating chocolate and sweets while you were supposed to be ill was not quite proper. This was made even worse by the fact that Bob had brought me the biggest Easter egg I had ever seen.

Phyllis's mother was kind, although she was of a more austere age, but I must confess I was terrified of her. She had a fur stole with glass eyes that she used to wear before she eventually took to her bed with the permanent vapours. When I was smaller I had been convinced it was still alive, and it still petrified me.

After three months I had made no great improvement, and I was in a very bad way. In fact, it looked as if I was not going to get better at all. Having tried all the available drugs, there was one other thing that might help me—surgery. This was a real risk. Even now surgery is dangerous and traumatic, but it was especially so in those days. And it might not work. But on the other hand, if they did not give it a try I would have to spend the rest of my life, which would probably be short, as a semi-invalid. For Bob, it was not much of a choice. I was a 12-year-old child, and my existence until then had been full of pain. He had brought me back to Ireland to end my suffering, and I think the idea of the alternative—to watch me waste away from TB and inevitably die too soon—hurt him deeply. Besides, Bob seemed to have great faith in my ability to overcome just about anything. We would give surgery a go.

The best part of my left lung had to be removed, and this procedure, 50-odd years ago, was cutting-edge stuff. No pun intended. The idea of opening someone's chest and playing around inside, and then putting it all back together again—hopefully with no spare parts—was a very new one. As I had been with streptomycin, so I was to be with this—an experiment.

The Brompton Chest Hospital in London was where I was taken for this latest adventure. Bob, being Bob and pulling strings, had managed to get the best surgical team available. They had carried out the same operation on King George VI a year or two previously, and he had since died. I took this as a bad omen, but I needn't have. The surgeon eventually got to be a knight of the realm for what he had done for the King— though he should have been equally honoured for what he did for me. He was a Welshman—Sir Clement Price-Thomas. I will never forget him.

I was there for about a week before the actual surgery, while I had a whole new round of poking and peering. For some reason, doctors never seem to believe each other's test results.

I was due to go to theatre on a Tuesday afternoon, at two o'clock. Once again my very life was in the hands of others, but this time I was old enough to understand all that was going on around me and exactly what was about to happen. I was terrified.

That morning Bob played canasta with me. It was a new card game and was all the rage. Bob always found it hard to give up his competitive instincts, and he did not even let me win. I did beat him at chess, but we were both pretty rotten at that game.

At two o'clock, I went to theatre. It was cold. Bob was there. The anaesthetist lowered his mask over my face; after that, I remember nothing.

Apparently, they woke me up while I was still on the table—to see if I would, in fact, ever wake again. When they opened up my chest, they found a much bigger mess than they had expected. There were a lot of lesions, which meant that part of my lung was attached to the chest wall. All that tissue would have to be cut back before they could even get to the part they were supposed to be removing. What should have been a fairly simple procedure turned out to be much more complicated. The two hours they had allotted stretched into five.

To make things worse, one of the team managed to put a nick in my pulmonary artery. The blood, Bob told me, was spewing out faster than they could pump it in. I still have a collection of little scars all over my body where they made cuts to find veins, so that they could get more blood into my body. Sir Clement, becoming desperate, told Bob that I was going to die on the table.

Bob, characteristically, didn't listen. 'Hitler didn't kill him,' he replied sharply. 'And neither will you. Do what you're paid to do.'

And he did. Sir Clement never was paid. I think that he was so surprised at my still being alive that he didn't have it in him to send a bill. However, Bob promised the surgeon that when I was able to go home, I would write him a letter on my birthdays. I never knew quite what to say in these letters, and I have the impression that they were extremely banal. But it is the thought that counts.

Even when I had been stitched back up again, things were not good. I was alive, and as far as my doctors could see the surgery had worked. But I was still very ill and my recovery was by no means a certainty. I began, slowly, to improve, but it was several months before I was well enough to leave London.

However, this time was not as disagreeable as it might have been. There were five men in the ward with me, and they took it in turns to try and get me to laugh. The nurses had told them to do this, the idea being that if I laughed, the remaining piece of my left lung would expand. For me, it was most painful, and never (until my latter days, perhaps) have I worked so hard at being grumpy. But these brave men worked at it with a will. They were a great bunch of guys. They all got better as well.

Mind you, they put me through a great deal of pain for their amusement. There was a tube in my side which was meant to drain the lung. One end went into my chest, and the other went through a suction pump into a large bottle on the floor. If the pump was on full, which it was supposed to be, it hurt like hell. Any time Bob came to visit, he would turn it down a bit—but the nurses would watch out, and as soon as he was gone they would turn it up again. I also found that if I breathed out as far as I could, I could blow bubbles in the bottle on the floor. This also hurt like hell, so I tried to avoid it, but the nurses let the others in the ward know that it was good for me. Every time one or another of them came into the room they would say, 'Blow us a bubble!' If I refused, they would tickle me mercilessly.

They made up for it, though, in other ways. Part of the treatment in this chest hospital was a bottle of stout in the evening and a portion of ice-cream, which was still rationed at that time. We would do a swap—my beer for their ice-cream. They got an extra beer between them; I got five portions of ice cream—a good deal indeed.

My stitches came out the very day I became a teenager. There were 26 of them; I kept them in a Vesta matchbox for years. Yet again I had escaped death, and yet again, it was thanks to the fact that I had the right people around me at the right time. I had the benefit of skill and dedication that I did nothing at all to deserve.

———•———

While I still had both lungs and was ill in the Square, some rather momentous things had been happening. John Huston, the film-maker, had the idea that he would like to make a movie about the Irish poet, Raftery. It was decided that the folk singer Burl Ives would be perfect for the part. Burl was six foot two and, while he was still bothering to weigh himself, over 20 stone. Doing anything near a convincing performance of a poet who was blind and not much bigger than me would surely have earned him an Oscar. The film was never made, but Burl came over to scout out locations. This involved a great number of pubs all along the coast, and a great deal of drinking.

Bob went to visit John Huston and, in his usual way of getting people to do his bidding, managed to get Burl to give a concert in the Gaiety Theatre for the Cerebral Palsy Fund, which was his project of the time. Bob's sister-in-law, Eirene Collis, was quite an authority on this condition and had managed to get Bob interested in it as well. In those days people with cerebral palsy were rather cruelly called spastics and quite often banished to the back room of the house. The fund was a great success and raised quite a large sum of money. It also did a lot to banish the ignorance that was current in Ireland at the time.

176

It was at this concert that Bob met Christy Brown. Bob saw him at the end of the concert, being carried aloft on a brother's back, and made enquiries as to who he was and where he lived. The rest, as the best books say, is history. After that, Christy got a lot of books to read from the Square and, most Saturday afternoons, on the way to Bo, Bob would call in to see him. I also went a few times—and like Christy, I had to be carried around. He and I would give each other grunts of welcome, which seemed to be all that was required. I remember he had a prank glass of whisky—you would turn it upside down and nothing would come out. Every time someone new would come into the room, he and I would give them this glass. And every single time, they fell for the joke. It was hilarious.

Bob gave Christy the encouragement and advice he needed to become a successful writer and they were firm friends for most of Bob's life. I think they had a bit of a divergence of opinion some time after the publication of *My Left Foot*, though—about Christy's next book. Bob felt that he was being a bit too free and easy with the vernacular of Dublin. The book should stand on its own merit, he thought; there was no need for these rather salty sayings. They did make up in the end, though, and Christy wrote a preface for Bob's autobiography.

Anyway, while Burl was in Ireland, Bob prevailed on him to come and visit me in the Square. And, by God, he did. He sat on the edge of my bed for hours and sang about the lady who swallowed the fly, the big rock candy mountain, the frog who went a-wooing, and all his other songs. He was enormous, but he had a very gentle voice and manner.

When I was in the chest hospital in London, Burl was doing his UK tour. By that time he had become extremely famous. He came into the hospital twice to visit, sat on the bed again and sang the songs. The hospital came to a standstill, and the best part of it was that some of his fame rubbed off on me. The five other patients in my ward could not understand how this famous entertainer would bother with the little Slovak who ate all the ice-cream.

From each city Burl played in during that tour, a gift would arrive for me. One of them was the *Eagle Book of Trains*. I had loved trains ever since my journey to see *Snow White* in Slovakia; this book and Burl's visits did wonders for my spirits. In fact, I am sure I got better much more quickly than I would have without them.

———•———

I missed an entire year's schooling while my chest was being dealt with—and another year of normal childhood. While I was ill this time there was another round with tutors, again without much success—and for this, again, I must take all the blame. At Newtown I had managed to become quite academic, but when I finally got back there I had missed the beginning of algebra, geometry, trigonometry and all the other new subjects of secondary school. I fell to nearly the bottom of the pile in academic terms. However, with great effort—though more of it was on the part of the teachers than myself—I was able to climb back up. With my usual lack of humility, I can say that by the time I finished school, I was right back at the top.

My TB finally settled down for good. There is no escaping the damage it did. I have various scars and deformities all over my body. But I have accepted them: they are part of me. There is a deep furrowed scar in my upper left arm, for example. It was caused by an abscess that formed when I was in Fairy Hill. Again I am lucky: if it had been half an inch lower, I would have lost the use of that joint. But that I have made my own. I used to tell my children that that's where I kept the vinegar when I was eating chips in bed. Salt in the bellybutton.

After that episode, the years and holidays went on. I divided my time, happily, between Newtown and Bo for most of what was left of my childhood. This part of life was nearly normal; though I wonder what it is that that word means. After the games with my chest and lungs, nothing of any great interest really happened—not to me, at least.

Within the family, though, lots of changes were taking place. When I was still at school, Edit left to start her nurse training. Despite her height, which is not very tall, she managed to become a very good nurse in Ireland and then in England, where she lived for a number of years. I think she enjoyed it very much—she always loved looking after people, and here was an opportunity to do that for a living.

Robby was by this time a medical student in Trinity College, and was courting a girl called Ivy who was from Singapore. Dermot had left for Canada, Edit was gone, and I had almost finished my time in Newtown.

I have been wondering how to write about this next part, but now I realise that there is no need to wonder. What happened happened; it is part of my story, an important part, so it will be told. While I was in London having my innards made outards, Bob had taken the opportunity to spend a good deal of time with Han, who was by then working in the East End, in the Jewish Hospital. Before he brought me home to Ireland, Han was pregnant with his son.

With a child on the way, and his other children pretty much set on their paths in life, Bob decided that the time had come for a divorce. This, of course, I am surmising—someone of Bob's class and character would never have dreamed of sitting me down and spelling it out. Anyway, I was still at an age where this was tiresome grown-up stuff. It was one day after lunch that Robby told me about the divorce. We were in the Square throwing a ball for Luke, a cocker spaniel, to catch. I remember thinking, 'So what?' It had nothing to do with me.

Phyllis, gracious and gentle as always, gave Bob a divorce and did not take him for every penny he had, which I dare say she might have done. Part of the agreement was that she could carry on living in the first two floors of the Square. She took in a few Trinity students, first of all as a favour to a friend and then as a bit of company for herself. I think it probably cost her more money than she ever made, but I think she was happy there.

When, in the end, it was time for Bob to retire to Bo, he needed a bit more ready cash to do it up. The Square was sold and Bob bought a charming little bungalow for Phyllis, just under Bray Head, where she spent many happy days walking her assorted dachshunds. Vicious little things they were, although I must take some of the blame, since I bought one of them for her. The morning I went to Bray to deliver it, it got hold of the back of my hand and would not let go. I was ringing the doorbell with one hand, while trying desperately to shake this thing off the other.

After the divorce, and when Bob and Han eventually returned to Ireland, he had lunch with Phyllis every Tuesday. So it was really a very civilised arrangement. However, I do remember one occasion when Phyllis had come down to stay with me. I had got a couple of whiskies into her, and she was opening up a bit. She leaned over to me and said conspiratorially, 'Of course, you do realise that she went out to get him. And she did.' Then, taking an extra-large swig, she said, 'And she's welcome to him!' This, of course, was most unladylike and most unlike Phyllis. But on many occasions when I would go and visit her I would bring a bottle. She would finish one drink, and then she would hold out the glass and say, 'I really mustn't.' So, of course, I would fill up the glass happily.

Phyllis was very good to me and Edit, and she was as good as she could be to her own children—but Bob overshadowed everything. That is the sort of person he was. Dermot, Robby, Edit and I—and Phyllis too—all accepted the fact. He was like Francis Drake or Walter Raleigh—an adventurer. Great on an open sea with the wind in his hair; less great in the small pond of family life. There was never any point in trying to blame him for his faults and excesses, in trying to change him or in holding him up for ridicule. Nor did I ever try to make excuses for him, because I knew they wouldn't wash. That was just Bob.

At the time of the divorce a few things were happening at once. Ireland was getting too small for Bob's talents and, if truth be told, probably for his 'I told you so's' as well. The Catholic Archbishop had been instrumental in getting a new children's hospital built in Dublin. Bob wanted the top job, and was very well qualified for it. But he was also a Protestant and had just got divorced. Before the days of equal opportunities, there was no way he was going to get it.

While this was going on in Dublin, on the other side of the world, Nigeria was gaining its independence. Bob happened to run into one of his former assistant doctors, who was from Nigeria and had always wanted Bob to go there and start a system of paediatrics. This man introduced him to Abubakar Tafawa Balewa, who was later to become Prime Minister of the new state. Bob immediately became friends with Balewa, and remained so. He was, in fact, one of the last people to see Balewa on the night he was murdered, some ten years later.[9] Bob was now offered a job setting up the paediatrics department in the university at Ibadan. It was not a difficult choice for him to make. He had a new wife and his son, Sean, had just been born. Here was a chance at a new and exciting beginning—an adventure. He was off like a shot, bringing Han and Sean with him.

After Bob and the others left, Phyllis and I would carry on as before. We spent the school holidays either in the Square or up at Bo. Phyllis, at almost 60—an age when a wheelchair would have been more suited to her—finally learned to drive a car. I was rather glad when my 17th birthday came and I was able to put the driving instruction that Robby had so patiently given me into practice. I got a licence and was able to take over the driving duties. I think Phyllis was also rather glad. She was a lady after all. I think she thought driving rather unseemly.

When I finished school I had moved permanently into the Square, and began studying for the matriculation exam for

Trinity College. In those days the school-leaving exam was not the big thing it is now. Anyway, at that time the ability to pay, rather than the ability to acquire knowledge, was the primary criterion for entry to these seats of learning. After a struggle, again with tutors, I finally managed to pass the exam and got a place in the School of Economics and Political Science. I didn't even know what Economics and Political Science was, never mind wanting to study it. I still don't for that matter. It was far too vague for me, far too abstract. I needed purpose, and I wasn't going to get it in Trinity. In the end, I decided that university education was not for me.

Bob had had an unshakable belief that I would go to university, and the last thing I wanted was to disappoint him. Even then I deeply appreciated what Bob had done for me and my sister, and I had a profound awareness of the fact that I was lucky to be alive, and that I was alive because of him. But notwithstanding the education in selflessness I received from the Quakers, I still had a tendency to think I was the centre of the universe—as, I suppose, do most young people who have just turned 18 and have the world open before them. As far as I was concerned, it was my life and I was not going to waste four years in useless study. So I declined the university's offer.

Bob and the family were aghast, and I got many a serious earful on the subject. They had all gone to university, and so would I. This was not on. There was even a letter from the family solicitor saying that the question of my allowance would have to be considered. Perhaps if he had used Hungarian I would have paid attention; as it was I gave it no heed.

I was not going to change my mind, but did my best to think of something else that might keep them happy. After deep and meaningful thought, I suggested that I might try hotel management. This was met with a rather cold silence. However, when I explained this would take place in the Shannon Hotel School, which had a very good name, and furthermore, that I would get a certificate, the idea became almost respectable. Almost. Bob eventually decided that boys would be boys and indulged my whim—although I think he was pretty sure I would be back inside the hallowed halls of Trinity within a year.

I got a place in the hotel school—probably because the Vice Principal was a Slovak—but I had to wait for a year. So Bob used his many connections once more to get me a job as a trainee manager in the Gresham Hotel in Dublin. He had looked after the son of the managing director at some stage or other, and called in the favour. I was shoved into the kitchen, and immediately found that I really enjoyed it, and was pretty good into the bargain. Here I was able to be creative and to give free rein to my imagination, as I had been at Bo. But also, as at Newtown, I had order. In the kitchen, everyone had their place and their function. It was sure, reliable, safe. This satisfied the desire for certainty that had been with me since Belsen. I decided I was going to be a chef.

I eventually got to the hotel school and then worked in

sundry hotels and restaurants—including Kilkea Castle, in County Kildare. This castle, inhabited since 1190, is the oldest such castle in Ireland. It used to be home to the Fitzgeralds— the Earls of Kildare and the Dukes of Leinster—who, as it happened, had a family connection with Bob. Sadly for me, it is too distant for him to have had any claim on the castle, but I always thought it quite a coincidence that Bob's little Slovak should end up working there as a chef.

It was a quaint place, a throwback to an earlier time, and it was famous for its ghosts. There used to be an old gardener, Dick, who had worked there all his life. He had a slight speech impediment, so was hard to understand, although I think he used to say the same about me. He always gave the impression of knowing a lot more than he ever let on, especially as far as the supernatural activity was concerned. You could pump drink into him all night, but ask about the ghosts, and all he would do was touch the side of his nose and give a big heavy sigh.

When I first went to work there I stayed in one of the blocks away from the main building. One of the old Fitzgeralds must have had a weak bladder, because I heard a toilet flushing every morning before dawn. There was no one else there but me. Big boy that I was, I always slept with the light on.

Bob used to tell a story of one of the times he visited the castle. At that time there were two very elderly Lady Fitzgeralds living there—Lady Emma and Lady Nestor. I believe, in fact, that they were the last of the family to inhabit the place.

Having taken tea with them, Bob asked Lady Nestor where he might find a bathroom. Lady Nestor lowered her head and replied, 'You'd better ask my sister. You know, she was married.' Such was that place.

———•———

Things chugged away merrily for a few years. I did some time in Switzerland, and did my best to learn the trade. This was before the days of nouvelle cuisine, where food is piled two and a half feet high on the plate and surrounded by miserable dribbles of balsamic vinegar. I cooked proper food, in proper portions with proper sauces. So long as you have fresh, good quality ingredients and simple ideas, you can eat well. I was never a brilliant chef, but I was always consistent, which is really much better than brilliant one day and rubbish the next three.

I also spent a year in Brussels. In Brussels I found myself a little Spanish girlfriend. I had no Spanish, and her English extended as far as *Twinkle, Twinkle, Little Star*, but not beyond. We had to use very bad French whenever speech was necessary. One evening, when we had been out, she nearly got the two of us locked up. We had had quite a few glasses of wine, and were walking back to her apartment, when we passed a very handsome red shiny sports car at the side of the road. She would not be satisfied unless I brought her home in it. She sat down beside it and refused to move. Perhaps inevitably, some large and fierce-looking policemen appeared and began to ask us questions in Flemish, of which I didn't understand a word. I hit on the words, 'Irish,' and 'Guinness,' which they seemed to understand and accept, as if they explained a lot. In the end I gave that girl up as too dangerous for my sensitive Irish heart. I wonder whatever happened to her.

I came back to Ireland after some time, and my mentor from the hotel school decided that I should try my hand at hotel management after all. He and some friends had bought a provincial hotel, and I was given the job of manager. Looking back now, I would say I was a hell of a lot better as a chef than as a manager. But I made the effort nonetheless.

Things were not too bad there until the nearby river flooded—and the hotel flooded with it. The water was five feet deep, and I was trapped upstairs when it happened. I ended up staying there for 36 hours, along with 12 guests and a few other staff members. The porter, who had been out when the water came in, had the right idea—he came to us on his hands and knees along a boundary wall with a bottle of whisky in each pocket and passed it up through an open window. I managed to cook a revolting stew on a coal fire. It tasted mostly of coal, but the whisky made it just about edible.

When the water eventually did go down, one of the owners came to see how his investment was. It was in an altogether sorry condition, and he quite clearly implied that it was all my fault that the river flooded and that I would be responsible for clearing up the mess. I, not unnaturally, told him where to stick the hotel, if it would fit, and said that I would be leaving. The other staff members, clearly suffering the effects of 36 hours of cabin fever, leapt to my defence. If I went, they went too.

That seemed to me a little drastic, the more so as Christmas was coming. In the end, wiser counsel prevailed for most of them and only one came with me. This was fair enough; she had a vested interest in me. Her name was Joan, and she became my wife.

———

Joan's family came from County Wexford, but as was typical in the 50s, they emigrated to England, and Joan was brought up there. She never did settle in very well across the water, and spent her childhood and later her youth travelling backwards and forwards between Ireland and England, staying with an uncle and aunt. We came from completely different backgrounds, but I have found that that, in fact, does not make a difference. Besides, I suppose, in a way, she too was a displaced person. Perhaps that had something to do with bringing us together.

She came over one summer and applied to me for a job in the hotel I was managing. I liked her at once, and took her on to work in the bar. We liked the cut of each other—quite a lot, as it happened—and before long we were keeping company, as it was called at the time.

Joan was impeccably loyal and extremely selfless, and we became closer and closer as the weeks and months went on. I had a very large teddy bear I was very fond of, which became a casualty of the flood in the hotel. Joan found it, washed it, dried it out and gave it back to me. She claims no recollection of this deed of kindness, but it is not the sort of thing I would forget. It sounds such an insignificant thing, but it is, after all, the insignificant things that make such a difference in these matters. After that, that was it, and before long we had decided marriage would be a good idea. I am not sure who brought up the matter first. That is the sort of thing I would not remember.

We began to make preparations. I had not even met Joan's parents yet and, being old fashioned, I had a notion of asking her father for his daughter's hand in marriage. We went over to England to see them. I was extremely nervous. This, as I saw it, would be my new life, my own family.

Joan's father must have wondered what on earth his daughter was letting herself in for. I tried to explain where I came from, and that I was really Irish, even if I did not sound or look it. The fact that I wasn't a Catholic was a lot for him to take in itself, never mind the rest of my tangled background.

He looked at me uncomprehendingly and a little suspiciously all the way through my speech—and when I had finished, he said nothing except, 'I think the dinner must be ready.'

After dinner, we went to the pub, and he was visibly dismayed that I did not get the first pint down in two goes. I must say, though, that in the end, after he got used to me, we got on very well together.

It was a small family wedding—in a Catholic church, of course. Bob and Han were still in Nigeria, so on my side only Phyllis, Edit and a few Collis cousins were there. Joan has lots of uncles and aunts, first cousins, second cousins, third cousins once removed and so on, who all turned up. I thought of the good room in Slovakia filled with chattering uncles and clucking aunts, of my own mother and father and my lost siblings. Would they have been proud to see their nephew, their son or their brother getting married? Would they have loved my wife as I loved her?

Years later, when one of my own daughters was getting married in Ireland, there were 120 guests, but only a handful of them were belonged to the bride's side. I remember thinking that perhaps this was what people meant when they talked about the legacy of the Holocaust. The uncles, aunts and cousins my daughter ought to have but does not. Isn't there something in the Bible about the sins of the fathers being visited on the children? Even unto the seventh generation. Except that my fathers had committed no sin. They were victims of the sins of others.

My marriage marked a transition for me. I was no longer a victim, no longer a sick orphan who needed saving. I was no longer in need of the succour of good people. I was healthy, educated and prosperous, and I was about to start a family—my own. I was able and ready to show those people who had been so kind to me what, thanks to them, I had become.

Part Three

—•—

The End

*Though I speak with the tongues of men and of angels, but have
not love, I am become as sounding brass or a clanging cymbal.*

—1 Corinthians 13:1

I N THE MIDST OF WRITING THIS book, I went to Adam's fourth birthday party. Adam is my first grandchild by my third daughter, Nichola. The grown-ups had a good time, although I am not too sure about Adam. I think he may have been a little overwhelmed by it all. This party was held in an auntie's house, a very nice house in the country. We had a summer's day, one of the few this year, so it was all lovely.

It has made me think about a few things. Most of the people there were Nichola's in-laws, but there were about 45 people there—which, in fact, is why the birthday boy was overwhelmed. Again, I thought of my lost family—my lost siblings. But maybe I had better rethink what I was saying about seventh generations. There was no deficit here; Adam has no shortage of uncles, aunts and cousins. Fair enough, my children and I are rather short on the relations—but the grandchildren, it seems, will be fine. I'm pretty sure the Bible says somewhere else, 'Go forth and multiply.' And so I have.

Nichola's husband has changed his name by deed-poll to Zinn-Collis. I am not exactly sure what his motive was, but I think I can assume it was not to steal my identity and defraud me on the internet. It means that the name will continue after I am gone. At these family gatherings the Zinn-Collis contingent will still be rather low in numbers, but is it not the quality rather than the quantity that counts? Besides, if Bob taught me anything, it is that you do not need to be bound by blood to be a family.

———•———

The flooded hotel apparently didn't fit where I had told the owner to put it, so Joan and I had to move on. There was a northern branch of the Collis family, who knew of someone building a brand new hotel outside Antrim town. Hotels need chefs, of course, and I duly got myself a job. To be honest, I was a bit out of my depth at the beginning, but two young chefs came from England to join me, and a bit of healthy competition spurred us all on. I worked there for about two years, during which time Joan and I had a daughter, Siobhan. She was born in 1967—a year and a month after we were married. Siobhan took a while to make her appearance—as, I think, is usual with first children. That was before the time when daddies witnessed the birth of their children. While Siobhan was being born, I was making myself very busy scraping paint off the walls of my first house and driving the hospital mad by phoning every ten minutes to see what had happened. She was the spit of my sister Edit when she was a baby. Absolutely.

Either I was very blind or very trusting, but I had no idea of the trouble that was about to erupt in the North. Antrim was then a small town, with quite a good mix of the two communities. One of the Northern Collises had been the Church of Ireland rector and used to play cards with his Catholic counterpart most Friday evenings. Apparently their respective flocks took their example and mixed with each other without any problems.

Thankfully, we did not stay there to see that change. Bob and Han were still in Africa, but their son Sean was now of school-going age, and they had sent him back to Ireland—to Newtown, in fact. One weekend I took it into my head to take Sean and some pals out for the evening, as you do for children in boarding school. Sean was a bright, gracious child, and he had Bob's spirit and sense of adventure. It was delightful to spend time with him. We stayed in a hotel in Tramore, outside Waterford, and I bumped into an old colleague who was working there. We got talking. There were greetings, plenty of drinks and plenty of reminiscences. And, as often happens in this line of business, he offered me a job. I accepted. We packed Siobhan and our baggage into the car, and down we came—just in time to miss the outbreak of the Troubles.

I stayed in Waterford for about a year, and it was after that when I started at Kilkea Castle—the ancestral home. The owner at that time, as it happened, was a survivor of Auschwitz. He had originally come from France, had moved to America and made lots of money there after the war, and had finally settled in Ireland. We worked together quite closely, and became friends. Each of us was aware of the other's background, yet we never discussed it. In general, until a very few years ago, very few Holocaust survivors did.

Joan and I bought a house in nearby Athy, and our second daughter, Caroline, was born. I was getting Sunday lunch ready, when I got a phone call to say that the baby was on its way. It was the quickest Sunday lunch I ever prepared. I got to the hospital just in time for things to get exciting. Caroline had, and still has, a lovely head of black curly hair, and she quickly acquired the nickname of Woollyhead. She has threatened to sue me for defamation if I mention that. I have pointed out, however, that if she sued me it would be for her inheritance, which I think has caused her to change her mind.

About two weeks after Caroline was born, something happened that made me a bit more grown up. Sean used to spend the Easter holidays from Newtown with a wealthy family, who were friends of Bob's and lived outside Waterford. That particular Easter Sean was involved in an accident, and he died. While he was playing, a wire got caught around his neck and he was strangled. He was only 14 years old.

The civil war was in full swing at that time in Biafra, and Bob and Han were there, up country. We couldn't make contact with them, and the mourning family now looked to me, as his closest available relative, to take care of things. So I made arrangements with the family solicitor. I said what should be done, and decided where the funeral was to be and when. We would bury him up at Bo.

Eventually, we were able to reach Bob and Han and give them the awful news. Various planes were held up at various airports between Nigeria and Dublin so they could make their connections, and they came home. When they finally arrived in Dublin, on the last flight that night, I met them at the steps of the plane. I shook Bob's hand, took Han's arm and did my best to comfort them both.

It is difficult to describe what I felt. I suppose I was grateful—grateful to the someone or something that enabled me to be there when it mattered to them. Up until then, they had been my constant supporters. They had been there for me when I had needed love and support. Now the roles were completely reversed. I was proud. I felt the rightness of the situation. These two people had gone through the war, Biafra, and all sorts of things, and now their bright-eyed boy was dead. How fitting it was that I, whom they had comforted through years of terror and torment, should now be there to comfort them.

After that, my relationship with Bob changed. I became not a ward, but a son. He had always followed his own law throughout his life, but after Sean's death he would telephone me and ask my opinion about things. That is not to say that he necessarily took any heed of my answers, of course—but it meant that in his eyes, I was now an equal.

Nichola, daughter number three, was born soon afterwards. She was healthy, and Joan was fine. This time I was there for the actual birth, and that was one of the most awesome experiences of my life. I saw it all happen. It was a nun who had said, 'Come on. You were there at the beginning, so you might as well be there at the end.' Not a very common opinion at that time, but an enlightened one nonetheless. I did not fall or faint or vomit or do any of those other silly things the Americans love to show us on television. I held the oxygen mask for Joan. Upside down. No doubt I was a great help.

Then I tucked Joan and Nichola up in bed and went home. There was no one still up to tell—and again, I felt the lack of uncles and cousins quite painfully. I had all this happiness, and nobody to share it with. God help me, I went to bed with a mug of cocoa. I felt very alone that night.

A few years later, the last one, Emma, was born. Just before the birth, the local GP had told me what to do if there was an emergency. I had told him that I had pulled a calf in my time, so I could probably manage a baby. Joan, who had been in on this conversation, was not too impressed, and I had to eat vast quantities of humble pie after that remark.

Emma was born in the morning, at quite a decent time—but the month was February, and one of the coldest winters we had had for years. Again, I was in the room when she was born, and I witnessed the whole thing. Well, most of it. This time I managed to kick the oxygen cylinder over, and by the time I got all the bits together again the best part was over and done with.

The first three knew what being a baby was all about. Put food in one end, let it come out the other, sleep a while, and then do the whole thing all over again. But not Emma. She knew about food in one end and out the other—knew that very well indeed—but she never seemed to get the hang of the sleeping bit. I can say with hand on heart that I did not get one entire night's sleep until Emma was a year and a half old. She would wake up in the small hours, howling. I would go in, make soothing baby noises and hold her hand. She would quieten down, and remain quiet until such time as I tried to tiptoe out of the room. Then all hell would break loose once again. She must have slept with one eye open. But I loved her as I loved them all, and although she no longer keeps me awake at night, that has not changed.

——•——

Bob and Han finally came back to Ireland for good, and retired to Bo. Bob's action-packed life settled down, and my own, too, was fairly uneventful. People came, were fed, and went away again. I spent brief periods of time working in various other hotels and restaurants—including a hotel in Tullamore in the Irish midlands, where we lived for a time.

Finally, Kilkea Castle came looking for me and made me an offer I could not refuse. Back I went. The ghosts were still there, of course, and no doubt still are, but they never caused me any great trouble. They say that it is only on the seventh day of the seventh month of every seventh year that the really spectacular things happen. Coaches in the courtyard, horses with silver shoes, wizard earls, and whatever you're having yourself.

One of these earls, the story goes, used to practise the black arts in a room in the tower. He was in this room one day—the seventh day, of course, of the seventh month—and turned his wife, whom he loved dearly, into a bird so that she could fly about. Just as all this was happening a cat came into the room. The wife flew out the window, never to be seen again. Old Dick the gardener, if you could understand him, used to tell it much better. In all my years in the castle—about 13 I think—that room was never let without the guest being told the tale at great length. Most of the time, though, it was used for the couriers from the coach tours, and they would get so drunk that it did not matter a lot to them what flew in or out the window.

When we had moved to the midlands Joan and I had sold the house in Athy, and going back to Kilkea meant moving back there. I managed to rent a bungalow in the countryside outside the town, to see how the girls would find rural living. I was all for it, of course—I must confess that I had ideas of a second Bo.

THE END

It was while I was holding the fort here, waiting for Joan and the girls to join me from Tullamore, that I had the first idea that there may be something wrong with me again. Having gone through so many variations of various illnesses, I have never in my life been quite sure what you were supposed to feel like when you were well. I still don't, for that matter. If I was huffing and puffing, which I was most of the time, I paid no heed. That, to me, was normal—though it did tend to scare the hell out of some people. I suppose they had terrible visions of having to give me the kiss of life, or something equally intimate.

If my body was misbehaving, I put it down to what had been. As I thought at the time, this was probably the best way to deal with my rather bashed-about form. If I had been of a mind to think of what had happened to it and to treat it accordingly carefully, I would have stayed in bed waiting for various bits of me to fall off. I would certainly never have done an honest day's work.

However, things began to happen to me that I could not ignore. One night I woke up and found myself unable to breathe. Shortly afterwards, this happened again. I had visions of kicking the bucket right there, in the middle of nowhere, and being found three months later, half eaten by mice. So reluctantly, I went to see my doctor. He, as you may well have guessed, was an old colleague of Bob's, a houseman from his Rotunda Hospital days. We had a chat, the way you do, then got down to business. Between us we decided that my new ailment could well be asthma. And after various tests, so it proved.

I must say that I was a bit knocked back by this news. I was 42 years of age, and since the fun with my arteries in London 30 years earlier, had never had a thought about my health. I knew that with my already weak chest asthma would be much more serious than in a healthy person.

However, it has not been the end of the world, and much worse things have since happened. And yet, I am happy to say, I am still here.

———•———

The idea of a rural idyll in the middle of County Kildare was a bit wishful on my part, as it turned out. My wife was from the city, and the girls had always lived in towns. I was working long and antisocial chef's hours, so to leave them abandoned to the weather and the wildlife was not the best of ideas. They hated it.

Eventually, we decided that country living was not for us and managed to buy back our old house in the town of Athy, which has been our home ever since. It was great moving back in. All the nails from the pictures were still there, and the furniture fitted in exactly as it had. Apart from the fact that the kitchen had been painted royal blue and the doors, as Siobhan called it, a Long Kesh brown, it was as if we had never left.

There our girls grew up into the fine and strong women they are now—with all of the joy that young people give their parents and very little of the pain they can put them through. I worked, and worked, and then I worked some more. I tried to be a good father and husband and, as with most of us, had varying degrees of success. I like to think I had more success than not. During this time Edit was working as a nurse in London, Robby had qualified as a psychiatrist, married Ivy and gone to live in Hawaii, and Dermot was in Canada. Phyllis was still around, living quietly under Bray Head with her various models of dachshunds.

Bob and Han were in happy retirement up at Bo. I visited them from time to time. Bob had written his autobiography up there, and he seemed to be enjoying farm life as much as ever.

It was 1975, and late spring. One Tuesday evening Bob went out on his horse, Tim, as he did most days. We had bought Tim as a stallion, and Bob had since had him fixed. He knew what he was missing, and I think he held it against us somewhat. Most of us had broken a bone or two by falling off him over the years.

Several hours after Bob left the house, Tim came back without him. Han and a neighbour immediately went out to the fields, searching. He had taken his usual ride across our land and some of the land of the obliging neighbours, so they knew exactly where to look. Soon, they came across the place where his body was lying. He was dead. Either he had fallen from Tim's back and had a heart attack from the shock, or he had had a heart attack and then fallen. Whichever way around, the result was the same. Bob was dead.

Han brought him back to the house and did what had to be done. She telephoned me with the news, and I arrived at Bo as soon as I could.

My first thought had been that there must be a mistake. Bob gone? It was impossible. It had seemed to me that there would always be a Bob. He would get old, certainly, perhaps forget things, tell the same stories twice—but he would always be there. This was a shock, a tremendous shock, and a painful one. I felt like any other son who had lost his father.

Han was, of course, very upset. She had laid him out in the usual manner, and had got a rhododendron flower and placed it behind his ear. He had been fond of the rhododendron bush. It had come to Bo from his old family home, and despite being eaten by the cattle every few months, still managed to produce a few blooms each year.

I was still in shock, which makes people behave in very strange ways. The sight of Bob with this flower behind his ear for some reason struck me as completely ridiculous. I don't know what he looked like, but it certainly wasn't a hula dancer. It was too much for me. I feigned a fit of coughing so I could leave the room before I burst out laughing. It was not that I did not care. I was grieving, deeply. My foremost protector, whom I loved, was gone. But the whole thing still seemed unreal.

Robby, who was on holiday in Jamaica at this time, came back the next day. Han brought him from the airport out to Bo, and I was there waiting. Having dusted himself down, Robby suggested that we should go for a drink. This was a momentous occasion, and on momentous occasions a drink was usually in order. I said no. Somehow it did not seem proper that we should leave the house as soon as he had arrived. I should have known better. Robby opened his doctor's black bag and produced dozens of miniature bottles of spirits. He would fill his bag on the various flights he took—and he was always a great traveller. So we had our drink—neat vodka—and felt much the better for it.

We arranged to bury him beside Sean. Han is there now and Phyllis is a few graves down. The service was simple and moving; we kept it a small affair. I belted out the hymns as loudly as I could—a bit nearer to the correct key than Bob would have, but with the same enthusiasm. He would have appreciated that. After some time, we had a memorial service in Christchurch Cathedral in Dublin, where Bob's many friends and former colleagues and patients were able to pay their respects.

When at last my incredulity wore off and a bit of thought set in, I felt that Bob's death was actually quite a relief. He had been such an active man, so vital and so energetic, that I hated to imagine him sitting by the fire with his slippers on, dribbling down his chin, his face covered in nicks from shaving. No, death would not arrive that way for Bob—not after his hero's lifetime. He died as he would have wished—in the outdoors, doing what he loved. And I am happy for him.

———

Throughout my life, until now, I had never spoken about my past. I had never spoken in any meaningful way about the war, the Holocaust, the concentration camps or displaced people. I did not consciously repress the memories; I never, like so many others, felt them well up inside me until they had to come out. I just did not think about what happened to me. I was busy making my own life, paying my taxes when I had to—which was most of the time—and raising a family.

Most people who knew me were vaguely aware of the fact that I was something called a Holocaust Survivor—and I must say that at times I have not been above using that fact. When I was working in Killarney, the head chef—and a very good one he was, too—was a German. We were working together one day, really quite hard. He had an expression he used a lot, which tended to come out when you were working well— 'That's the shpirit that von the var.' When he said it this time, I could not resist the urge to round on him and say, 'Who the hell won the war?' Having this vague knowledge of where I had come from, there was a very long pause before we went back to work again. But what could he say? To be honest, I had a lot of respect for that particular man, and I think he might have returned the feelings. But I was a cocky little upstart at that time. Franz, I am sorry.

Another time, one of the gas ovens was playing up, and a wedding party was due to arrive, By now I was head chef, and taking the responsibilities of my position seriously, I pushed the underlings out of the way and announced that I would fix it. And so I did, in a manner of speaking—but not until I had managed to blow the doors open, break my glasses, and get myself a nice cut on the face. The wedding had to wait. A waiter who was standing behind me was not very impressed by my efforts. He looked at the doors, looked at my broken glasses, and then at my bleeding face. Eventually, he turned and went off to do whatever it was he should have been doing anyway, but as he went he muttered, 'Jaysus, Collis, if the fucking Nazis didn't get you, we will!'

I was so surprised by this remark that I did not have it in me to pull rank and tell him a thing or two, like the importance of having respect for the head chef. Actually, he brought me to town to see a doctor, and then to a pub to settle my nerves. We had to have two drinks, for custom demands that you buy your round. The wedding party still had to wait; luckily, they were fine about the delay and most solicitous when the situation was explained to them—the explosion bit, not the pub bit.

My own family were, by and large, unaware what their dad was all about, for even to them I had never spoken about where I had come from and what had happened to me. In the early years, when the girls were young, I felt that the knowledge would be a burden to them—and besides, how could they understand it? Then I went down the road of not wanting them to feel any different from other children their age. Fitting in at school is always difficult enough, and they had slightly darker skin than most of the other children, which already marked them out. Then, as they got older and I did too, it just seemed easier not to bring it up. They ought to know—of course they ought—but I suppose I hoped they would pick up a bit here and there.

Neither have I ever really spoken to Joan about Belsen. It was never a secret, but my reasoning was that marriage was difficult enough without bringing more baggage into it. If words should pass, and we all have them, how easy it would be to use what happened to me as an excuse. A pretty unfair one, of course, but irrefutable. A passport to unconditional sympathy and the absolution of all my sins.

I have always thought that playing the Holocaust card could be a good way to acquire a mistress, though she would probably run a mile if she knew what she was getting into. Of course, I have never tested the hypothesis, and I think it is too late now. The bump on my back has ceased to be an attraction, more than likely because I have managed to get a bump of equal size on the front as well.

How the human mind deals with such suffering as I went through is a question for psychologists, and not for little Slovaks. But looking back now, I think that for all my good intentions, the real reason I did not speak probably was only partly to do with protecting my wife and daughters. The main reason, most likely, is that I was afraid of what I might find in my head.

In fact, a very many of the survivors of the Holocaust have had the same experience. Throughout our lives many of us have attained varying degrees of normality. We have managed to repress, or avoid, or escape the horror we have witnessed—to bury it like garbage in a landfill and to build our lives on the shaky ground above. Not all of us were able to construct lives of sufficient solidity, and those who were not able have been taken by mental illness or depression. But others among us survived for 50 years without having to acknowledge our terrible past.

Fifty years on, we survivors had become set in our ways. For the most part, it was too late for our characters to be altered; our families were by and large grown and gone; our responsibilities had all been fulfilled. We were able, finally, to bring our past to the forefront of our minds, to see it for what it was and to narrate it to the world.

———•———

During the early 1990s I was working in a golf club outside Carlow—very posh, as Emma would say—and one day I got a phonecall from the local radio station. Would I like to do an interview as a bit of local interest? This was before *Schindler's List* reawakened curiosity about the Holocaust, and there was no great knowledge about it in Ireland, never mind in Carlow.

I was not sure how my family would react to hearing me on the radio. They are rather like the people I had a fear of when I started to write this. Would they parse what I said, analyse it—and judge me? I thought they might well try to put me up for adoption. And my family's opinion aside, I would have to talk to a stranger on the radio, for the entire county to hear. However, I had a few phonecalls with the reporter, and decided to give it a try. What followed came to me as quite a surprise, and I am not sure if I am the better for it yet.

The reporter's name was Helen. She was good at what she did; she had done her homework, and knew exactly what to ask. She made me feel comfortable and realised when a particular subject was making me uneasy—though not many, as it turned out, did. So I 'came out'.

I found that speaking about my experience was easy. I was articulate, confident, and I seemed to get through to people. What's more, I felt immeasurably better for having done it. After that interview, I was greeted with a few odd looks, and hundreds of questions from everyone I met. 'Do you have a number tattooed on your arm? What did the gas smell like?

212

Were you ever tortured?' Many of the questions were none too intelligent. Anyone who knew what the gas smelled like, for example, would not be around to talk about it. And there is not much point in torturing a child of four—the Nazis would have realised that someone of that age would not have any great knowledge of army manoeuvres. But I bore these questions with as good a grace as I could muster.

Helen moved to RTE, where she is now, and did a further interview. This time she included Han, Suzi and her brother Terry, and she even managed to find Miss Barcroft—the sweet little old lady who used to bribe me with sweets to learn my colours in English. This was the first time I had seen Suzi since that day in Fitzwilliam Square when Rusty had stolen her cake, and I had been so amused.

A short while after this, I came up with the notion that it would be a good idea if someone recorded something of Han's life. If anyone was worthy of a biography, she was. She was getting on in years and I had the feeling that time was running out. If this was going to be done, it had better be done soon.

Helen came to the golf club one Sunday for a spot of lunch, and I mentioned this to her. She was most receptive to the idea, for of course she had met Han and felt there was a lot to be said. Helen put the idea to her producers, and they came up with an even better one. How about taking Suzi and me back to Belsen?

I had a long, hard think, as did Suzi, about this notion of revisiting the scene of so much pain for both of us. Like me,

Suzi had only begun consciously to think about Belsen in the recent past, so of course neither of us had thought of going back. If we did, what would we stir up? Perhaps more than we would be able to handle. Was it worth taking this chance? Sleeping dogs did cross my mind. Yet, I had a feeling that here might be my chance to lay some ghosts to rest. I felt that I had to confront the past fully, the better to speak for the ones who cannot. And for that I had to go to Belsen.

First of all, the film crew came to the very posh golf club so that they could see what a chef gets up to. I was supposed to be working and talking at the same time. Some would say that I should not mix the talking with the cooking, but then again others would say I should not mix the cooking with the talking. Suzi had an easier time; she just had to sit at home. They also came to my house, and Gizmo, my cat, got to make his television debut. It could be this which has given him ideas above his station.

It was arranged that we would go during the last weekend in February. We had to fly first to London, and then to Hanover, which is the nearest airport to Belsen. Poor Helen had to be minded, as she is not mad about flying. But Suzi and I looked after her, and she did not need counselling, or trauma therapy.

The first night I spent mostly on the floor of my room. As soon as we landed I found myself gasping for breath, and down on the floor seemed for some reason to be the only place I could get some air. My breathing, ever since I had developed asthma, had been pretty iffy. Don't forget that I had most of a lung missing, and to my eternal shame I had been a smoker. In the morning, with the help of a local chemist, I was able to stock up on inhalers. I think that RTE decided it would be cheaper to buy these than to have to ship me back in a box.

After we got home, Caroline, who is quite interested in alternative medicine, said that this was all caused by emotion, which governs the chest. I will concede that she may have had a point on this one; the old emotions, at this stage, were all over the place with the thought of what was about to happen.

The next morning we walked through Hanover before catching a train to Celle, the nearest town to Belsen. We were being filmed all the time and were doing our best to look pensive and profound, although the pensive part was not too difficult. Not surprisingly, the nearer we got to Belsen, the quieter our mood became. Both Suzi and I were with our thoughts, wondering what we would find, how we would feel and how we would react. It would be fair to say that the fearlessness I had felt at the start of this adventure was rapidly leaving me. It is all well and good to talk about the past, as I had done, but to be faced with the prospect of coming face to face with the subject matter was another thing entirely. However, it was too late to change my mind.

Even now, trying to describe this, it is still giving me pause. I shall not burst into tears or any such thing, for it is not good for the keyboard, but I will take a break now. Six years ago we made this journey; the feelings are still with me.

So we got to Celle, and from there we took a taxi to Belsen. When we pulled up outside there was a bus disgorging itself of a load of young students. They were all chattering and laughing and generally having a good time, the way you do when you are out from school for the day. I thought of another bus that had pulled up in the same spot over 50 years earlier. I found myself in quite a state.

I wiped my nose on the back of my sleeve, no doubt the way I used to do there before. Giving myself a gentle talking to, and taking a few gulps of air, I made my way in. Can a place have a feeling of evil? Or is it the people who have the feeling and put it on the place? I cannot say, but a feeling of evil was sure as hell there. We all felt it.

I had no sense of anger, blame, condemnation, or any of those other sentiments that great atrocities of history produce, though maybe I should have. I felt only loss, desolation, and the sense that I was alone.

There is nothing there. There are no huts, no cookhouse, no latrines. The gallows which was outside our hut, to the left, is gone. There is only a large clearing of dead grass with pine trees around the edge. And, scattered around the area, the graves. Long, low mounds, varying in length according to the varying numbers of bodies buried beneath them. They are two to three feet in height, covered in sleeping heather, which will wake up in the spring and perhaps bring a bit of colour to the place. For now it is all greys and browns. No birds, no colour, no life—but the reminder of death in great measure.

On the side of each mound there is a message in three languages. Here lie the bodies of 500, or 1,000, or 2,000, or 3,000. Who knows for sure how many were there, under the earth? Who was counting as these corpses were being bulldozed or thrown like sacks of potatoes into the pits? The dignity of the dead was sacrificed, during the first few days of liberation, for the sake of the living—as it had to be.

Suzi and I went to one of the graves, quite a large one, and looked at it. Then we looked at each other. The body of her mother, as well as mine, was in one of these pits. 'What now?' I said to her, 'What do we say?' It was hard. We placed a few pebbles on the grave, as is the Jewish custom, and Suzi lit a candle. We moved apart, each with our own reflections and our own misery.

The camera crew, with a great deal of tact and understanding, left us alone for a while. We needed the space and the time, for the tears of 50 years were flowing. This had been a miserable place; now it was miserable and bleak too. All the vegetation was dead along with the many thousands of people, invisible under the ground and rotten almost out of existence. Vegetation comes to life again, it renews itself each year. What of the souls sleeping in the ground here?

Do they awake? Do they come alive again in a place called Heaven? Or do they sleep forever under the sleeping heather? I have no answer. I have long since ceased to look for one; it is beyond me.

———•———

We left Belsen in a very much more sombre mood than the one in which we had arrived. Suzi, it would be fair to say, was shaken. Helen, the producer and the German film crew were shaken too. What had seemed at the beginning like an interesting television documentary ended up being a rather powerful experience, for them as well as for us.

For the rest of the trip I was very much turned in on myself, as was Suzi. We had not known what to expect and so we had not been prepared for our own reactions. The experience had hit us both, hard.

My breathing, which had been bad, was not any bit better by the time we arrived home. No doubt it was my emotions again. The producer arranged a wheelchair for me when I was being whisked from one terminal to another. I must say I felt a bit like the Queen Mother as the crowds parted in front of us, and I gave a limp-wristed regal wave as we passed the peasants. There was another wheelchair at Dublin Airport, but this time the crowd was not so eager to part. The puffing was now of Thomas the Tank Engine proportions, but in Dublin, unless you have two legs sticking out in plaster, or are shrivelled and bent double, wrapped in a rug, you have no business in a wheelchair. So I kept my regal limp wrist to myself.

I am still undecided as to whether or not it was a good idea to go back to Belsen. It disturbed me, perhaps more than I care to admit. Yet having gone, I am glad that I did so, for it has made me face up to things, to acknowledge where I have come from and what I have lost. The trip did not satisfy me; it left me feeling just as empty as when we got there. It did not bring closure. You learn to live with what happened, but you are alone, and you are empty. There can be no closure on the Holocaust.

———•———

When I returned from Belsen, I had a day or two at home and then went back to work in the very posh golf club. All the huffing and puffing was refusing to abate, but I was putting it down to my lifetime companions—smoking, that bit of asthma, my missing lung, and my newest companion, old age. These were just being aggravated by the fact that I was under stress from the trip. It would pass.

I had been lucky throughout my life, but it seemed to me

that I must be down to the last few of my nine lives. I blamed anything I could think of rather than entertaining the notion that I might be seriously ill yet again. I only managed a day and a half back at work, however, before my breathing became so strained that I had to call the emergency services. I was taken off by ambulance in the middle of the night.

The hour was so late that there was no traffic and therefore, sadly, no flashing blue lights or wailing sirens. Little boy, will you ever grow up? Caroline's husband works in Dublin and was on earlies that particular week. He was driving and happened to catch sight of me, in the back of an ambulance, with a mask over my face. When we turned off for Peamount Hospital he had a fair idea as to what was going on. He waited as long as he could, for this was about four in the morning, and then at seven o'clock phoned Caroline. Without knowing it, I was causing great consternation all over the place.

Peamount Hospital is one of the old TB sanatoria of the 40s and 50s. It still has a TB ward, but for the most part deals with people like me—huffers and puffers. Nonetheless, it is one hell of a fine place. When I arrived there I created a great deal of fuss, as I usually seem to, for the place is not used to emergencies, and most people there arrive during office hours. I was finally settled, only to be woken an hour later by a large man playing American country music at full volume on his whatever-it-was. I was having a very hard time trying to keep breathing. I was very uncomfortable and very annoyed, and after a few hours of worn-out horses, feckless wives, smoking bears and all the other mainstays of American country music, I suggested to the man that as I was not too well, he might care to turn down the volume a bit. Well, not in so many words. I have been as honest as I can be in this tale, so I had better continue. While my voice was Fitzwilliam Square, the terms I used were pure farmyard. Bo again. He turned the damn thing down for all of five minutes.

For the next ten days I was poked, prodded and bled as is the custom. They x-rayed me to see what they could see; they oohed and aahed over my medical history. Eventually, they let me go home with a few more pills to take. I was not better, but I had kept on badgering them to discharge me until they had given in, with the offer of a bed any time I needed it.

When I got home, I slept on the floor or in a chair. My long-suffering wife never knew where she would find me in the morning, or whether I would be breathing when she did. I was very ill; everyone knew it. In fact, I knew it too, but I had some foolish idea about keeping a stiff upper lip. Perhaps that was Bob's influence.

I stayed at home for a month or so. Eventually, my legs had become the same diameter from my thighs to the ground and there was fluid building up in my chest. A dozen paces or so was the best I could manage. I was sick, and finally, I confessed to it. I wanted to go back to hospital.

Back in Peamount, after more poking and prodding, they gave me all sorts of medical names for what was wrong with me, including CCF—congestive coronary failure. In simple terms, though, my lung was giving out and was being followed by my heart. I was more or less drowning in my own body fluids. I also had diabetes. I was seriously ill. I tried not to think of cats and lives.

There was a great deal of concern among my family. Some of them had been up with some jelly babies to see me, and were told upon their departure to prepare themselves for the worst. Caroline phoned Robby in Hawaii, and Robby, to his eternal credit, dropped whatever he was doing and came over.

Some of the family came up a few days later expecting to see their father laid out, but they found me sitting outside in the sun having a dispute with one of the nurses who was trying to put sun block on me. I was having none of it. She won, of course.

When Robby arrived he was able to swap long words with my doctors, and they came to the conclusion that I was in fact getting the appropriate treatment. There was concern that I had been retaining fluid—I was not peeing as much as I should. There was, to my way of thinking, a rather unhealthy interest shown in each millilitre of fluid I was able to deposit in a little jug. I felt rather like a small boy being potty trained.

However, one day I started and thought I would never stop. My little jug was full to overflowing, and the joy shown by the staff was to match. This was the start of my getting better, whatever better is for the likes of me. For the rest of my time in Peamount I would spend the nights in a chair, wrapped in a blanket. The night staff would come along and think I was asleep until they saw my arm waving at them. I must confess I did enjoy trying to scare them.

As I continued to mend, I was let out for an afternoon, and then for a weekend. Eventually, I went out on bail. Again they assured me that there was a bed if I wanted it. It is still my hospital and I go there on quite a regular basis, which is a bit like going back to boarding school. Everything is always just as you left it. In an odd way that is very comforting. I used to see my consultant there about four times a year, and was always greeted with the same phrase—'My God, are you still alive?' Of course, I always had to answer, 'Yes—despite your best efforts.' If you are going to be ill, I cannot think of a better place for it.

They told me to try to work for a half a day or so, when it was quiet, to see what would happen. In a kitchen, though, quiet is a scarce commodity, and there was no way I was able to cope with work as a chef. So I was declared an invalid.

What was I to do? After 40 years of constant activity I had no employment, and my mobility was pretty limited. I very much missed work at first. I had not expected to have to leave, and the change was too sudden. As always, though, I adjusted to the situation I found myself in, and before long I was thinking about how I could use it.

This time, though, I would exploit my newfound leisure not for my own benefit. After I had started speaking about Belsen on the radio and on television, people had begun to approach me to speak in schools, colleges and universities. Since that first radio interview the idea had been present in my mind that I was one of the last witnesses to one of the most momentous events of recent history. Many people more clever and learned than I am have already recorded the facts, of course, but I was actually there. I am a witness to both the evil of the Holocaust and the saving love shown by Bob Collis and so many others; I am a product of both that evil and that love. It became clear to me that I had and have a duty to tell my story before I die.

One of the first things I did was to buy a computer, with a vague view towards trying to put down some of my deep and meaningful thoughts. I should have got some lessons first. I had it for about three months before I worked out the ironic fact that if you want to finish, you have to click on 'Start'. I used to turn the thing off by pulling out the plug. Then, of course, I would get nasty messages on the screen when I turned it back on. Also, pictures of young ladies with a severe deficit of clothing used to keep appearing on the screen, promising all sorts of things a good clean-living invalid should know nothing about. Not good for my heart, nerves, blood pressure or immortal soul.

I am still not sure I have the measure of the computer. Sometimes I think it works me rather than the other way around. One of my recurring nightmares is that everything I have written will disappear. But my daughters understand these things and usually manage to get me out of most of my technological messes. My instructions from Caroline are: whenever and wherever I see the word 'Save', say yes, and stay the hell away from the button that says 'Delete'. That, I have found, has been very sound advice and I have followed it to the letter.

I also joined the local branch of the Samaritan movement. This is something I find very fulfilling, and it tends to put my own life into context. It has taught me that none of us knows the half of what people are feeling. The world, historical atrocities aside, can be an awful place, and what is one person's little nuisance can be another person's cross. I am being Christian again, which I do not mean to be, but those are pretty good terms for describing this. Bob would have been mad at me for saying that. He always said, 'Find your own words. Your story, your words.' Lay off the songs and the Bible, in other words.

Working with the Samaritans, who are all shapes, ages, and sizes, has reinforced the basic trust in humanity that was given to me by Bob. It is a great movement. And that sort of work is good for me, because it is about listening, not talking. We do not give opinions; we try and draw out from the people who call us what they themselves feel is the solution to their problems. I am not looking for any kudos for the little that I do with the Samaritans. I am lucky in that I have the time and apparently I have the skills to do a bit of good. I am anything but an angel, and I do not wish to pretend as much, but I feel very strongly that it is my duty. I have been given so much in this life by way of help, encouragement and advantage, that I have to put something back. I have come under the influence of so many good Samaritans that it is only right that I should attempt to become one myself. I have not decided whether God, or Allah or Jehovah or Buddha, is up there, but working with the Samaritans is my way of saying thank you to whatever it is you say thank you to.

And of course, I have continued to speak about Belsen, to anybody who will listen. Joan and the girls are now quite bored with the entire topic, and will beg people not to get me started. But, as they will say, I am a man on a mission. My work is now the business of letting people know what my life has been about. Sometimes the kids in the schools I visit get emotional; sometimes I do too. In the documentary that brought me back to Belsen, I can be seen snotting all over the screen. So what? This is necessary. For the horror of the Holocaust to be real to us, we must feel it.

I am no longer an invalid, for I have now reached official old age. I still cannot do any work, and I live on other people's taxes. For a number of years now, I have been in receipt of what I call my pension, from Germany. They call it reparation, for damage to my health. All I have to do is present myself at the German Embassy in Dublin once a year with a passport, to prove that I am still alive, if not well. When I first started to do this, the people working there were the same generation who would have been involved in the war. There always seemed to be a feeling of embarrassment among them at my presence. I would be pushed into a side room, the necessary stamps would be applied to the forms, none of which I understood, and then I would be ushered out. After a few years had passed, and the next generation took their place, my reception seemed to be somewhat more hostile—sadly, in fact, rather as some of us in Ireland are to the immigrants and asylum seekers we have now. 'What do you want?' their expressions asked. Another sponger on the state. So as soon as the stamps had been stamped, I would usher myself out as fast as I could. Now I deal with the grandchildren of those people involved in the war, and the attitude is much more laid back. No shame, and no resentment—just part of the day's work.

That is right and proper, I think. We cannot carry on with this blaming and this guilt forever. I do sometimes wonder, though, whether we are letting go too soon—lowering our guard and leaving ourselves vulnerable for the same sort of thing to happen all over again. I have forgiven the German people for what they did—or for what they did not do—60 years ago. And they have forgiven me, or so it would seem, for reminding them of the shame of their parents. But we must be careful lest we forget too readily. Perhaps we must feel fully the evil of the past—on one side, shame; on the other, injury—in order to learn from it.

In the schools, the knowledge the younger ones have about the Holocaust is very mixed. They all know something about Anne Frank, of course, and are very impressed when I tell them we were in the same camp. But many of them have very little idea as to what actually happened. We have had so many wars since, so many other holocausts, that perhaps this is not surprising. However, I often feel that our children should know more than they do, and I am determined, in the years I have left, to do all I can to tell them. Those of us who were there are getting fewer and fewer, and so our responsibility is great.

The rest of my time is taken up by my family, whom I adore—and who, I hope, adore me. The people who looked after me throughout my life have all gone now—except Edit, who has retired from nursing and lives in Bray. She is still true to our mother's request that she mind me, and has extended it to her nieces and her great-nephews and great-niece. She has never once forgotten a birthday or special occasion, and has been enormously generous to us all. She used to send expensive clothes from England for the girls, which were the height of fashion. All the other children on the road would be green with envy. I believe she would gladly give any one of us her last penny. I think she is proud of my children, and me, and proud of what she has done with the responsibility our mother gave her.

Phyllis died in 1993; Edit and I were both with her when she died. Her mind had gone by the end, and I found it distressing feeding her bits of orange the way I do my baby granddaughter. But she knew nothing about it, so it was not so bad, I suppose, and again, we felt it was proper and fitting that we should be there for her. Han followed her just a year ago, in the same way. They are both buried with Bob up at Bo—a confused and confusing set-up, yes, but none of us who are involved would have it any other way. We were all so intertwined in life that it should not be any other way in death. It is my wish to end up there as well. It is so peaceful that the calm of the grave would be better there, I think. The girls, though, have said that I will have to die in the summer, for they have no intention of driving up there in the middle of winter.

I have had vague thoughts over the years of trying to find whoever is left of my original family in Slovakia—of filling up my car with compact discs and blue jeans and motoring off to the Tatra. These thoughts never came to anything. What if I did find them? There would be tears and hugs in different languages—but not in English, which is the only one I can still understand. Tears I don't mind, but as you may have gathered, I do not do hugging very well. Besides, after all these years my uncles and aunts would certainly be dead, and my cousins would be complete strangers. What would we have in common? And would they have any interest in seeing me anyway?

No, there is little there to be achieved, and besides, my family is here. Between my wife and me is the warmth of 40 years and a well of companionship and comfort. I do not think she knows how much I value the rustle of the newspaper and her sighs when I get up and down out of the chair for the 17th time, but I do.

My daughters have grown up into very different people, and I am proud of each in a different way. They can be dangerous when they are together. They have four identical pairs of socks that say, 'Girls on a mission,' and they meet in each other's houses every now and again, and large quantities of drink disappear.

A few years ago, Robby came over from Hawaii and Caroline cooked a family dinner. They decided they would have baby Irish coffees, which is coffee liqueur with Bailey's on top. Poor Robby couldn't handle it at all. After an hour or two he gave up and went home. Quite often at these occasions they end up fighting the bit out. And yet, they are very loyal to each other, and God help anybody who looks sideways at me or their mother.

How they grew up to be normal, with me keeping such a rein on them, I do not know. I suppose I always had it in the back of my mind that I had lost one family, and was going to do all I could not to lose another. Perhaps that was selfish; I was extremely possessive of them and I acknowledge that. Mind you, I think I loosened up as they grew. Caroline tells me that I actually shoved her out the door when she was going to her first disco. So in the end, it seems that I became a smart daddy and knew when to look the other way. I don't know, but whatever I did worked. They are fine women and I love them all very deeply. If they read this and are embarrassed by their father, it will not be the first time, and anyway, they need to know it.

For all the years I had with Han and Bob, they never mentioned where or how they found me and my sister. Now that I am older and not a great deal wiser, I feel that I would have liked to talk to them, to let them know how grateful I am. But as so many of us do in these sort of circumstances, I have left it too late. I will not make the same mistake with my own children.

I have grandchildren, too—Caroline's son Tony, who is just coming up to his 18th birthday, and Nichola's two—Adam and Molly. Adam is four, and Molly has just turned one. The latter two drive me up the walls because they are children and they are noisy, but I am mad about them.

For no particular reason, last week I just sat back and watched Adam doing things at home. His daddy is very good with his hands and has a toolbox, and Adam has a toolbox of his own. He was going around the house with a measuring tape, measuring whatever he could find, and he was as happy as can be. He is four and a half—the same age as I was when I was taken from my home and tossed into a concentration camp. Watching him, I found myself feeling extremely frustrated with the world. How can we let such things happen to children of that age?

And watching my four-year-old grandson pottering in his ordinary innocent way around my home, I was struck, once again, by how lucky I am. I have a family, a normal family; coming from where I came from, I think that's quite an achievement. But the achievement is not mine. I owe their very existence, never mind what happiness we all have, to the people who shared their family with me and gave me the opportunity to make my own.

Joan and the girls, too, deserve their share of the credit. I cannot help but think that if I hadn't had this wife and these four children I would not have turned out as reasonably normal as I have. I think I probably owe them a lot, because their very presence helped me to be what I am. And of course, I must include the cat in this, whom I also love—even if he does take the bigger half of my chair.

EPILOGUE

I HAVE COME TO TERMS WITH what has been, and I have been able to function quite well, or so I think. But it would be disingenuous to make out that having been cast into a concentration camp at the age of four, and left to die, I have suffered no lasting ill effects. There is my sorry physical state, of course. But with a bit of navel gazing, and trying to be honest, I must acknowledge the mental effects, too.

I do have a fear of anyone or anything getting too close. Whether this is the real me or a protective shield I have built up around myself I can not say. Despite it I have functioned; I have even been quite successful—materially, socially and emotionally. But I wonder what Joan and the children would say about me, if they were being honest. Have I been cold and distant, inward-looking, unemotional? Have I buried my head and tried to ignore things I should have shared?

I have perhaps kept an important part of what is me all to myself, hidden a large portion of my personality from the world. That is to my detriment. It is a misuse of those who matter most to me. They trust me and deserve that I should trust them. And without fully trusting those closest to me, perhaps I have been prevented from becoming a complete and rounded person. I remember thinking when I was a lot younger that I was a displaced person, a refugee, and somehow unclean and unwanted. My heart has been scarred by these feelings, but my intellect tells me that my displaced status was of my own invention.

I hope I have not made myself out to be anything special. It is tough, this business of humility. But as I said at the beginning, I have not done anything of note in this life. All I did was survive, and even for that I cannot take credit. I owe it to whatever it is that made me an enchanting scrap of humanity, to whom people responded so well, and to the undeserved goodwill of many good people. I have had an extraordinary experience, it is true—but I am a very ordinary man.

There are many things I do not understand about myself—and, by and large, I do not seek to explain them. I am what I am, and I am what I have been made. I think a large part of the reason why people such as myself manage to survive is that we take things as they happen, shrug our shoulders, and get on with the next bit.

I have bashed away at my computer, getting mixed up, preaching and giving out like a grumpy old man with a stick and a flat cap—confusing you and myself, for there are so many things I am trying to say.

I have tried to put down what it is like to be me. I have

tried to remember the dead—my mother, my father, my older brother and my baby sister. Although I was too young really to know them, my grief for them is real. None of us can know the lost millions of the Holocaust, but I hope that in telling the history of one family, I can express grief for many, and for the pity of their destruction.

Grieving, though, is looking backwards, and I have wished as well that we should endeavour to look forwards, and not to let the same sort of thing happen again. At that we are not doing very well, for there have been many instances of the same bloody mess in many different countries, and still not enough people have been able to say, 'Stop.'

I have told the story, too, of some of those people who did say, 'Stop'—who did stand up against the evil that they saw, and despite their faults and weaknesses did the best they could to give life back to some of those from whom it was stolen. If this book does nothing other than show up the good we are capable of as well as the evil, it will be worthwhile. How true it is that a disaster will make the front page of a newspaper, whereas a story of kindness may, if there is nothing better, make an inside left page. I have told of the horror because it needed to be told. What happened to us was too hard, too savage, ever to forget—and the happiness I have managed to salvage does not make it less so. Perhaps we need to keep some of it, for we all need a past. Like a story, life must have a beginning, a middle and an end. And what is a story without a beginning? This tale, however, is much more the inside of the paper than the front page—but joy, care, kindness, happiness, charity and love are worthy of being read about.

I suppose what I have really tried to express is love in its broadest sense—which encompasses the love of humanity, the love of self and the love of family. The individuals who beat us, who killed us and who abandoned us to disease must have had their own mothers, fathers, children. But they were able to lose sight of them. In Nazi Germany, love in its broadest sense was buried by an entire nation. And, love being absent, an opposite force was able to take over. Then those others came along. Bob, Luba, Han, Phyllis, and so on—who had faults enough, but had love enough between them to restore the balance.

So, the cowboy with the white hat and the white horse has got the blonde and is getting ready to ride into the sunset. The fat lady is doing up her stays and is getting ready to sing, so we must be coming to the end. As I finish, though, I will put down a few lines of doggerel which came to me one day when I was having a bath—that is, when I was still able to climb in and out of the bath. Now it is all showers, and I must face the fire hose daily—but by now, thank God, Allah, Jehovah, Buddha or whoever is up there, I am big enough and ugly enough to handle it. These lines are for my children to read at my funeral, whenever that may be. They say that the way I am going, I will outlive them all. Despite my nine lives and my tendency to land on my feet, I am not inclined to believe them.

There will be no Nobel Prize here, but I hope that these lines will show the essence of what is and has been us. And then the fat lady can start.

> When I die will it be with a lion's roar or a kitten's
> whimper?
> Will it be with the thunder of drums or the clanging of
> a cymbal?
> When I die will you remember me for what I am, what
> I was, or what I might have been?
> When I die, shed but a little tear—not for you and not
> for me, but to comfort the neighbours.
> You and I will remember the fun, not the gloom and
> the might-have-beens.
> Think of the walk on the beach, the scare in the car, the
> overdue haircut, the bursting trousers,
> For this is what was, is and shall be me.
> The drums and cymbals are of no import,
> For I made you, and you made me, and I am.

Notes

———•———

1 On 30 September 1938, Britain, France, Italy and Germany signed the Munich Pact, under which the Sudetenland—the western area of Czechoslovakia—was ceded to Germany. The other signatories believed that this would perhaps satisfy Hitler's rage for *lebensraum*. Instead, he invaded the rest of western Czechoslovakia several months later; since the main Czech defences were in the Sudetenland he met little resistance. He also persuaded Fascists in the east to declare an independent Slovak state—which effectively came under Nazi rule. In 1939 many anti-Jewish laws were brought into effect and the deportations of Czech and Slovak Jews began during that year. By the end of the war, all but 20,000 had been deported and most of these had perished at Auschwitz.

2 About 50 miles north of Berlin, Ravensbrück opened in 1939 and housed 900 women prisoners. By 1945 it contained more than 45,000. The prisoners were subject to slave labour, horrific medical experiments, sterilisation and periodic selections, after which those considered too weak to work were shot or sent on to Auschwitz. In 1944, a gas chamber was built in Ravensbrück, in which thousands were exterminated before liberation.

3 The largest and most notorious of the Nazi camps. As well as a concentration camp and about 40 satellite labour camps at Auschwitz, there were four vast gas chambers disguised as showers. Prisoners were exterminated using a pesticide known as Zyklon B, which produced deadly hydrogen cyanide gas when exposed to air. There were also four crematoria in which their bodies were incinerated. Although the SS destroyed much of the evidence, estimates suggest that up to one and a half million people, mostly Jews, were exterminated here.

4 The most infamous death march took place when, days before the Russian Army reached the camp, the Nazis evacuated Auschwitz. 60,000 prisoners were marched 35 miles to a transport station to other camps. A quarter of this number did not survive the journey. Since the 1990s, people from all around the world have taken part in the annual March of the Living, where hundreds of Jews and non-Jews walk from Auschwitz to Birkenau to commemorate the Holocaust and to teach people about the dangers of racial and religious intolerance.

5 Kramer had been an electrician before he joined the Nazi party in 1932. He worked at Dachau and Auschwitz, where he conducted selections. He was promoted to commandant of Belsen at the end of 1944, and imposed such a harsh regime that he became known as the Beast of Belsen. He was a rigid proponent of orders, bureaucracy and discipline, and remained in the camp until the British arrived, while the rest of the SS fled before them.

6 SS Irma Grese had grown up during the time when Nazi fervour was conquering Germany. She had become a fanatical supporter of the regime and its ideology and after leaving school at age 15, entered

240

an SS sanatorium as assistant nurse. She soon volunteered to go to work in the concentration camps, trained at Ravensbrück and was subsequently transferred to Auschwitz. There she was responsible for the physical, emotional and sexual abuse of prisoners, and nicknamed the Beautiful Beast. She was also reported to have taken both Kramer and Josef Mengele, the infamous Auschwitz doctor, as lovers. In March 1945 she was moved to Belsen and continued her career of brutality until she was captured by the liberators in April.

7   The trials were based on the Geneva Convention's recommendations on how to treat prisoners. Kramer's defence centred on his cold and amoral view of the situation. He simply did not think about the condition of the inmates, and viewed their starvation and neglect as his duty, according to the orders he had been given. He was found guilty of war crimes and was hanged with ten others on 12 December 1945 by Britain's chief hangman, Albert Pierrepoint.

8   Grese was sentenced to death for her part in the Final Solution and hanged by Albert Pierrepoint on 12 December 1945. She was 22 years old when she died.

9   Balewa's government had been dogged by regional unrest and in January 1966 a coup staged by a section of the army finally overthrew him. Balewa was kidnapped and killed; his body was found on a roadside near Lagos several days after his death.

FURTHER READING

Collis, Robert and Han Hogerzeil, *Straight On*, London: Methuen, 1947.

Collis, Robert, *The Ultimate Value*, London: Methuen, 1951.

Collis, Robert, *To Be a Pilgrim*, London: Secker and Warburg, 1975.

Doorly, Mary Rose, *Hidden Memories: The Personal Recollections of Survivors and Witnesses to the Holocaust Living in Ireland*, Dublin: Blackwater Press, 1994.

Lewis, Helen, *A Time to Speak*, Belfast: Blackstaff Press, 1992.

Shephard, Ben, *After Daybreak: The Liberation of Belsen, 1945*, London: Jonathan Cape, 2005.

INDEX

THE LEBANON DIARIES

AN IRISH SOLDIER'S STORY

by Martin Malone

Martin Malone has the army in his blood. After five terms in Lebanon between 1985 and 1998, he is ready to tell his amazing story. He's seen it all, from the terror of battle and the sight of children patrolling the streets with rocket launchers to the tragedy of many a colleague's death and the disappointment at missing the birth of his second child.

Serving as a Military Police officer for the UN, he has seen the best and worst sides of army life. He put his life at risk repeatedly in one of the world's most dangerous places, but has come up against endless difficulties and opposition from his own army.

He fought a successful and high profile compensation case against the army, while his novel about a soldier further ruffled feathers until he felt forced to quit his career.

This is his story as he wants it to be told. He pulls no punches, revealing the side of the army we don't see and showing how many honest men have been treated by other soldiers and by the state itself.

It is a must read for anybody interested in the military in Ireland.

To order this book go to www.maverickhouse.com

MUNSTER RUGBY

THE PHENOMENON

by Eoin Murphy

The Heineken Cup is the holy grail of Irish rugby. This intensely fought competition pits provincial clubs against European teams on an international stage.

One club more than any other has dominated the tournament since it began. This club and its legions of loyal fans have experienced both heartache and exhilaration in the quest to win the league. Now Munster Rugby is the pride of the Irish, the champions of the 2006 Heineken League.

Journalist and provincial rugby player Eoin Murphy examines the meteoric rise of Munster Rugby, their history and what makes the club truly unique. Using interviews with legendary players, commentators and die hard fans, Murphy gives a unique insight into this special rugby club.

From the impenetrable fortress of Thomond Park to the sealed dome of the Millennium stadium in Cardiff, the book recounts the club's road to success and tries to uncover exactly what makes the club the phenomenon it is.

This book is a must read for every rugby fan.

To order this book go to www.maverickhouse.com

SIEGE AT JADOTVILLE

THE IRISH ARMY'S FORGOTTEN BATTLE

by Declan Power

The Irish soldier has never been a stranger to fighting the enemy with the odds stacked against him. The notion of charging into adversity has been a cherished part of Ireland's military history. In September 1961 another chapter should have been written into the annals, but it is a tale that lay shrouded in dust for years.

The men of A Company, 35th Irish Infantry Battalion, arrived in the Congo as a UN contingent to help keep the peace. For many it would be their first trip outside their native shores. Some of the troops were teenage boys, their army-issue hobnailed boots still unbroken.

A Company found themselves tasked with protecting the European population at Jadotville, a small mining town in the southern Congolese province of Katanga. It fell to them to try and protect people who later turned on them. On 13 September 1961, the bright morning air was shattered by the sound of automatic gunfire. This was to be no Srebrenica. Though cut off and surrounded, the men of Jadotville held their ground and fought...

To order this book go to www.maverickhouse.com

HEROIN

A TRUE STORY OF DRUG ADDICTION, HOPE AND TRIUMPH

by Julie O'Toole

Heroin is a story of hope; a story of a young woman's emergence from the depths of drug addiction and despair.

Julie O'Toole started using heroin in her mid-teens. A bright young girl, she quickly developed a chronic addiction and her life spiralled out of control. Enslaved to the drug, Julie began shoplifting to feed her habit before offering to work as a drug dealer for notorious gangsters. Julie was eventually saved by the care and support of a drugs counsellor, and by her own strength to endure.

Heroin is a tale of how a young girl became a victim of circumstances. Julie's story takes us from Dublin's inner city to London and America, and gives an insight into how anyone can become a victim of circumstances.

With honesty and insight, Julie tells of the horror and degradation that came with life as a drug addict, and reveals the extraordinary strength of will that enabled her to conquer heroin addiction and to help others do the same.

To order this book go to www.maverickhouse.com